I FOUND IT!

I FOUND IT!

The Story of Bill Bright and Campus Crusade

Richard Quebedeaux

Published in San Francisco by **Harper & Row, Publishers**

NEW YORK   HAGERSTOWN   SAN FRANCISCO   LONDON

FIRST EDITION

Designed by Jim Mennick

Library of Congress Cataloging in Publication Data

Quebedeaux, Richard.
  I FOUND IT!

  Includes bibliographical references and index.
  1. Bright, Bill. 2. Evangelists—United States—Biography. 3. Campus Crusade for Christ. I. Title.
BV3785.B73Q4   1979   267'. 61'0924 [B]   78-20582
ISBN 0-06-066727-3

---

79 80 81 82 83 10 9 8 7 6 5 4 3 2 1

The member of the Body of Christ has been delivered from the world and called out of it. He must give the world a visible proof of his calling, not only by sharing in the Church's worship and discipline, but also through the new fellowship of brotherly living. If the world despises one of the brethren, the Christian will love and serve him. If the world does him violence, the Christian will succour and comfort him. If the world dishonours and insults him, the Christian will sacrifice his own honour to cover his brother's shame. Where the world seeks gain, the Christian will renounce it. Where the world exploits, he will dispossess himself, and where the world oppresses, he will stoop down and raise up the oppressed. If the world refuses justice, the Christian will pursue mercy, and if the world takes refuge in lies, he will open his mouth for the dumb, and bear testimony to the truth. For the sake of the brother, be he Jew or Greek, bond or free, strong or weak, noble or base, he will renounce all fellowship with the world. For the Christian serves the fellowship of the Body of Christ, and he cannot hide it from the world. He is called out of the world to follow Christ.

DIETRICH BONHOEFFER, *The Cost of Discipleship*

Contents

Preface

If we are to believe the pollsters, the mass media, and the evaluation of many prominent religious leaders, the United States is currently experiencing an evangelical revival of major proportions. The word *evangelical* comes from the Greek *euangelion*, good news, and has been used widely in Protestantism since the Reformation to describe that school of Christianity centered on salvation as a gift of God appropriated by faith in Christ—good news indeed. In modern-day America it has come to refer to, in particular, a Christian who affirms the full authority of the Bible as the Word of God written, who has made a personal commitment to Jesus Christ as Lord of his or her life, and who believes in *evangelism*, the act of proclaiming and demonstrating the good news to others in the hope that they too might believe.

In 1976, a Gallup Poll indicated that 34 percent of all American adults had been "born again," that is, had had a turning point in their lives marked by a commitment to Christ. Among Protestants, the figure was 48 percent of those polled; 18 percent of all Catholics surveyed also admitted that they had been born again. Evangelical Christians are now to be found almost everywhere—in politics, the entertainment industry, professional sports, big business, even in the predominantly secular academic community.

Whatever the totality of reasons behind this evangelical revival, one very important contributing factor has surely been the practice of evangelism among evangelicals themselves. And most prominent among the "professional" promoters of Christian evangelism today—

aggressive evangelism—is Bill Bright, founder and president of Campus Crusade for Christ. For Bright and his 6,500 staff members in ninety-seven countries, evangelism is not an avocation nor even a vocation; it is a lifestyle. The dedicated Campus Crusader focuses his or her energies almost completely on "winning, building, and sending" men and women into the world for Christ so that they, in turn, might win, build, and send still others. Bill Bright probably raises and spends more money on evangelism than anyone else, and he is regarded, even by the liberal *Christian Century*, as one of the most influential religious leaders in the United States today.

Because of the vast amount of money raised and spent each year by Campus Crusade, its extensive use of the media (in the "I found it!" campaign, for instance), its unabashed aggressiveness in evangelism, and the "politics" of its president, Campus Crusade and Bill Bright himself have become extremely controversial in American religious life and, in fact, in religion throughout the world. Furthermore, there is a certain mystique about Bill that filters down into the movement he directs, a mystique that makes it hard for the outsider (and some insiders as well) to fully understand his goals, his strategy, and—more important—the vision that compels him to move forward relentlessly despite criticism and despite cost.

This is the first comprehensive treatment of Bill Bright and Campus Crusade undertaken from the "outside." In discussing Bill's life and thought and the movement he founded, I have sought diligently to make both understandable—to break stereotypes—and to indicate not only the strengths but also the weaknesses that together contribute to their contemporary significance. Although I have tried hard to be objective in my evaluation, no worthwhile treatment of the subject can be totally unbiased, and I have my biases. I am an evangelical myself, and I believe in evangelism. An author without this conviction would probably have written an entirely different book. Bill and his staff cooperated with me fully, answering all my questions frankly, completely, and, in my opinion, honestly. Without this cooperation the book surely would have taken on a different character. Nevertheless, except for numerous lunches, breakfasts, and dinners, a free ticket to the Athletes in Action–

University of San Francisco basketball game in January 1978, a paid-for night at the Washington (D.C.) Hilton, and complimentary blank cassette tapes and books written by Bill and Vonette Bright, I was in no way "bought off."

Campus Crusade did set up interviews around the country for me with—quite clearly—some of their best staff members. But to balance that, I also spoke with a number of other present and former staff whose opinions were often somewhat at variance with the more "official" assessments I was getting at the same time. Not *much* different, however. During the past several years I have had some rich working relationships with a few Campus Crusade personnel that, naturally, have colored my thinking about their "boss" and about the movement they represent. And I must admit that a good number of the Campus Crusade people I interviewed and got to know personally—white and black, male and female—are among the nicest individuals I have ever known. Yet despite these self-confessed biases, I very much hope that this book still offers the fair and balanced evaluation of Bill Bright and Campus Crusade I originally intended.

I would like to thank all those members of the Campus Crusade staff and those outside the movement, too numerous to mention here, who assisted me in this project and even made it a top priority in their work. Most especially I want to thank my editor, Roy M. Carlisle, whose relational genius was the key factor that led to the book. It was his idea in the first place, and he made it happen.

RICHARD QUEBEDEAUX

Nevada City, California
September 1978

PART I
ROOTS

1 Bill Bright the Boy and Young Adult

Next to God we are indebted to women, first for life itself, and then for making it worth having.

CHRISTIAN N. BOVEE

"He's generally quite serious. You can see the gears moving in his head—constantly. When he asks you a question, you feel like he's looking for more than just an answer; he's also trying to find out who you are, what you're feeling, how involved you are in the work at hand. Soft-spoken, low-key, no flash. He gives the impression of having a good sense of humor, even when he isn't attempting to be funny. He's been known to tell extremely corny jokes . . . and to forget the punchlines. Solid like a rock." So goes the characterization of Bill Bright by one of his most discerning colleagues—a trenchant description of one of the most misunderstood Christian leaders of our time, a man both revered and despised, honored and belittled, praised and criticized with the same intensity by friend and foe.

Like Franklin D. Roosevelt, he stirs up the emotions to the point where you either love him or detest him. It's hard to stand on neutral ground when the name Bill Bright comes up in a conversation. And there's a certain mystique about the man, too, that even some of his closest associates and confidants have been unable to penetrate; for just when you think you've broken through to his heart and soul, you discover that there's more, much more, to be learned about him and what makes him tick. If you *have* seen the gears moving in his head, you know that they never stop long enough to let you put him in a mold fashioned by human hands. But then you remember the

Apostle Paul's words, "Don't let the world around you squeeze you into its own mould, but let God re-mould your minds from within, so that you may prove in practice that the plan of God for you is good, meets all his demands and moves toward the goal of true maturity" (Romans 12:2, Phillips). With that, you finally begin to understand who Bill Bright is and why he does what he does.

EARLY LIFE IN OKLAHOMA

Coweta, Oklahoma, is a town in America's heartland. Like Plains, Georgia, it is the home of the rugged individualist—where you can do it, and more than that, you can do it on your own. It's a world of right and wrong with no in-betweens. If it's worth doing at all in Coweta, it's worth doing right. Here the American Dream is a reality. Hard work, might makes right, Horatio Alger, up by your bootstraps. Bill Bright was born in Coweta to Forrest Dale and Mary Lee Rohl Bright on October 19, 1921.

Bill speaks with great affection about his mother and his boyhood in Oklahoma. "Mother had a remarkable conversion experience through the Methodist Church when she was about sixteen. She was always the first one in our family to wake up, and she would begin each day by reading the Bible and praying. I was born on a ranch with four brothers and two sisters. We were very busy all the time. We worked hard, and, really, we didn't even know anyone who didn't work hard. It was a great life!" He goes on to relate how "Mother always began her day with the Lord and walked with him every waking moment. She would sing quietly, hum softly, hymns of praise to the Lord. I assumed that all mothers were like that, but now I know that she was probably one of the unique mothers of our time."

Bill gives his mother the credit for being the most influential person in his own spiritual growth. "She was a very humble, quiet, gracious woman. I have never seen her do an unkind thing, never heard her raise her voice in anger, never heard her criticize anyone. Mother lived for her children and for our neighbors. She had been a school teacher before marrying my father and had a great appreciation for literature. With seven children in the family, almost always one of us was writing a book report for school. Mother would read that particular classic to all of us as the family gathered round. At mealtime she was always the last person to eat, because she wanted to be sure that everyone else was served first. Mother would eat what was left over. We lived five miles from the nearest community. Many times I would walk or run home from school, and she would walk a mile or two from the house to meet me, as she did with the rest of the kids. Then we'd stroll back together and talk about what was on our mind."

Bill received much of his sense of morality from his mother. "She was always doing something for someone in need. From her I learned to appreciate people of all races. In Oklahoma there were blacks who did not have the privileges we enjoyed. But Mother always reminded us that we were no better than anyone else, that we should never look down on anyone no matter what the color of his or her skin, and that we should never feel inferior to anyone else. That's been my philosophy from the beginning, even though I wasn't a Christian in my youth." Mary Lee was sick most of the time she carried Bill and was at the point of death on many occasions. "She dedicated me to the Lord, but I didn't know that until years later, because Mother didn't want to influence me. She wanted *God* to influence me."

Bill Bright was a hard worker indeed and a very ambitious young man. While he was a student at Northeastern State College in Oklahoma, his gifts of leadership quickly became apparent. Bill was editor of the college yearbook and student body president. Listed in *Who's Who in American Colleges and Universities*, he received his Bachelor of Science degree in 1943, and shortly thereafter was already teaching extension students as a member of the faculty of Oklahoma State University.

LIFE IN CALIFORNIA

But Bill wasn't happy just teaching. He wanted to make money. So, like the multitudes of Oklahomans before him, Bill moved to Los

Angeles with fortune in his eyes. "I worked twenty-four hours a day at my business, Bright's California Confections, which marketed its fancy foods—fruits, candies, jams, jellies, and other epicurean delights—through exclusive shops and the major department stores in the United States and Canada. I was dedicated to making a fortune. In my youth, Dad had been a materialist, and I followed his example. I desperately wanted to 'make it big,' to be a success. And I was on my way. Nothing could stop me, so I thought, but how wrong I was, because the God I didn't even acknowledge was already working in my life the day I arrived in L.A."

Bill spent his first evening in Los Angeles looking for a good time. He found it, even though what he found wasn't exactly what he'd been looking for. Bill picked up a hitchhiker who turned out to be a member of the Navigators, the well-known evangelistic organization whose work centers on Scripture memorization. This hitchhiker also happened to be living with Dawson Trotman, founder of the Navigators, and his family. He invited Bill home with him for dinner and to spend the night. The Trotmans treated their guest with a great deal of hospitality, and Bill still remembers their warmth. Later that evening, Bill went to a birthday party for Daniel Fuller, who had just come home from the Navy. Dan is the son of the late Charles E. Fuller, the famous radio preacher and founder of Fuller Theological Seminary in Pasadena, where Dan is now professor of biblical interpretation. In time, Bill Bright and Dan Fuller became close friends.

Hollywood's First Presbyterian Church has been one of the foremost Protestant congregations in the United States. Its senior ministers have been some of America's greatest preachers, but even more important is the fact that it has spawned a whole generation of eminent Christian leaders. When Bill first came to Los Angeles, Louis H. Evans, Sr., was pastor of "Hollywood Pres." A dedicated agnostic, Bill Bright had no time for church. He was making it in business and had an amateur radio program on Sundays, after which he would regularly go horseback riding in the Hollywood Hills. However, an elderly couple Bill met took a liking to him, and whenever he saw them they insisted that he go to Hollywood Pres. to hear Louis Evans preach. The couple's persistence finally got the best of him.

"I don't know how it happened," he relates, "but on my way back from the stables on one occasion, with my riding clothes smelling like a horse, I slipped into the back row of the church and sat down. The service was already in progress. I stayed awhile but walked out before the benediction. I didn't see anyone, and, quite frankly, I didn't *want* to see anyone." Nevertheless, Bill's name found its way to the church's young adult group, and they invited him to a party. "We had a great time. It was in the very luxurious barn of an actor who was associated with Hollywood Pres. I met a lot of wonderful college students and grads who were happy people. They weren't getting drunk and carousing around, but they *were* having a good time." Bill was impressed, and he continued going to church activities in the months that followed.

Hollywood Pres. soon became part of Bill Bright's life. "Later I met a group of older people in the church who were very wealthy and influential. I was attracted to them initially because I, too, wanted to make money and be a success. But here were people who were already successful, and they loved Christ. In fact, they were much more excited about him than about their palatial homes and bulging bank accounts." Bill still has fond memories of the swimming parties he attended with his Hollywood Pres. friends at the mansion of one of the prime developers of the exclusive Bel Air district. "His home was always open. I would go there with many others. We would eat his delicious food, swim in his pool, and listen to conversations about Jesus Christ."

Like the other young adults in the church, Bill also began to study the Bible. Nurtured by Christian fellowship, the preaching of Dr. Louis Evans, and the teaching of Henrietta Mears, the remarkable woman who was then director of Christian education at Hollywood Pres., he finally allowed God to influence his life, thus fulfilling his mother's fondest desire. "I studied until I was at a place where I was ready to receive Christ. But nobody ever talked to me personally. It was about that time that Dr. Mears was speaking about Paul's conversion on the Damascus Road. She ended her message by saying to us, 'When you go home tonight, get down on your knees, and say with the Apostle Paul, Lord, what would thou have me do?' Well, I did exactly that. It wasn't a profound prayer, but the Lord heard it, and he changed my life—not dramatically in an instant, but gradually."

And so Bill Bright "the fancy foods man" became a Christian. There was no Bible-thumping preacher, no fire and brimstone, not even an altar call—just the simple invitation of a saint whose "boys" in the Hollywood Pres. college department have become some of the most highly respected Christian leaders in America today. It is extremely difficult to understand Bill Bright without reference to his mother and her profound influence on his life. Henrietta Mears must also be seen in a similar light, for without her help and encouragement Bill probably would have become just another successful businessman.

HENRIETTA MEARS

Henrietta Mears had an inclination for the impossible. "There is no magic in small plans," she said. "When I consider my ministry, I think of the world. Anything less than that would not be worthy of Christ nor of his will for my life." Born in 1890 in Fargo, North Dakota, she was the daughter of a wealthy banker, much of whose affluence she inherited. Having graduated in chemistry from the University of Minnesota, Mears became a high school teacher and principal. A very gregarious woman, she taught speech and dramatics as well as chemistry. She was also an active member of the First Baptist Church of Minneapolis, then pastored by the highly influential W. B. Riley.

One Sunday when Riley was out of town, his pulpit was filled by Stewart P. MacLennan of Hollywood Pres., the preacher who single-handedly had turned a "little country church" near the corner of Hollywood and Vine into one of America's great congregations. After the service, MacLennan had lunch with Henrietta and her sister Margaret, and so began a relationship that culminated in Henrietta Mears' appointment as director of Christian education at

Hollywood Pres. When she arrived there in 1928, the church's Sunday school had an enrollment of 450; two and a half years later, the number had grown to 4,200.

"The first thing I did in Hollywood was to write out what I wanted for my Sunday school. I set down my objectives for the first five years. They included improvements in organization, teaching staff, curricula, and spirit. I wanted a closely graded program, teaching material that would present Christ and his claims in every lesson, a trained teaching staff, a new education building, choirs, clubs, a camp program, a missionary vision, youth trained for the hour." All of Mears' plans for her Sunday school were eventually realized, and by the 1950s she had become almost a legend in the ministry of Christian education. Henrietta Mears was a founder of the National Sunday School Association, and, in 1933, she established Gospel Light Publications (now based in Glendale, California), one of the world's foremost publishers of Sunday school curricula.

When most people think of Sunday school, they think of children. But Henrietta Mears also had a great influence on college students. Bill Bright emphasizes the fact that "she knew how to inspire young intellectuals." Mears taught the college class at Hollywood Pres., where hundreds of students from the campuses of greater Los Angeles came to hear her teach each Sunday morning. She was proud of her students, a number of whom she had "sent" to Harvard and Yale. Bill was an active member of her beloved college department (which included graduates as well). He became its president and chairman of its "deputation teams" (mission task forces), in which he spent five years working in Los Angeles' skid row rescue missions and local prisons. Scores of Mears' boys went on to seminary and became ordained ministers. She also founded and directed what in 1949 became know as the Hollywood Christian Group, a weekly Bible-study fellowship at her mansion that included such celebrities as Roy Rogers, Dale Evans, Tim Spencer, Connie Haines, Dennis Morgan, and Virginia Mayo.

In 1937, Henrietta Mears purchased the old Forest Home resort in the San Bernardino Mountains of Southern California for $30,000 and turned it into a nondenominational Christian conference center.

Forest Home has been noted for its annual "college briefing conferences," envisioned originally by four of the Mears boys (Bright was one of them) and begun in 1947. The idea was to gather and inspire college students ("brief" them, as soldiers had been briefed before their missions in World War II) to "win the world for Christ." Eightly-seven colleges and universities in nearly every part of the country were represented by the 600 students in attendance at the first briefing conference. A little-known evangelist from the South was invited to speak to the 1949 conference. His ministry had not been going well, and he agreed to come only with great reluctance. But the young southern evangelist had a kind of second conversion experience while walking alone in the woods at Forest Home one evening. It was shortly thereafter that Billy Graham launched his first Los Angeles crusade, and the rest is history.

Henrietta Mears did not have an earned doctorate. Although Bob Jones University awarded her an honorary Doctor of Humanities degree, she always preferred the simple title *Teacher*. She never married but lived most of her life with her sister Margaret, who managed her finances until the latter died. Bill Bright describes Teacher's character aptly: "She had amazing vitality and enthusiasm about life. She was not a beautiful woman physically, but she possessed such charm and such enthusiasm and such a love for Christ that she appeared beautiful to all of us who knew her. She was a woman who ministered in the power of the Holy Spirit." Reflecting on her impact on his own life, he goes on to say, "She knew how to reason; she was a logical thinker and *very* convincing. A gifted writer and speaker, she led many people to the Lord. Nobody ever taught me how to witness, but I observed her on numerous occasions and picked up ideas just from watching her. I've known many ministers and Christian leaders, but, frankly, I've never known anyone who led more people to Christ following a Bible class or a message." The late Clarence Roddy, who was professor of homilectics at Fuller Seminary, used to say that Henrietta Mears was the best preacher in Southern California. She was not ordained and had no formal theological training, but the impact of her life and teaching on her boys was comparable to the influence some of the world's greatest theologians had on their students.

In 1947, Henrietta Mears gave the opening address at the first Forest Home college briefing conference. Afterward, she and four of her boys drew up a pledge, which they incorporated under the title, The Fellowship of the Burning Heart. The name was based on John Calvin's seal, which shows a hand offering a heart on fire, around which is the inscription: "My heart I give Thee, Lord, eagerly and sincerely." Bill Bright was one of the formulators of this pledge, which reads in part:

> I am committed to the principle that Christian Discipleship is sustained solely by God alone through His Spirit. . . . Therefore I pledge myself to a disciplined devotional life in which I promise through prayer, Bible study, and devotional reading, to give God not less than one continuous hour per day. (Psalm 1)

> I am committed to the principle that Christian Discipleship begins with Christian character. Therefore I pledge myself to holy living, that by a life of self-denial and self-discipline, I may emulate those Christ-like qualities of chastity and virtue which will magnify the Lord. (Philippians 1:20, 21)

> I am committed to the principle that Christian Discipleship exercises itself principally in the winning of the lost to Christ. Therefore I pledge myself to seek every possible opportunity to witness and to witness at every opportunity to the end that I may be responsible for bringing at least one to Christ every 12 months. (Matthew 28:19; Acts 1:8)

> I am committed to the principle that Christian Discipleship demands nothing less than absolute consecration to Christ. Therefore I present my body a living sacrifice, utterly abandoned to God. By this commitment, I will that God's perfect will shall find complete expression in my life; and I offer myself in all sobriety to be expendable for Christ. (Romans 12:1,2; Philippians 3:7-14)

Bill has never repudiated this early pledge. In many ways it was only the first concrete expression of a commitment that would eventually take on far greater proportions.

SEMINARY

A major event of Bill's life during the years immediately following his Forest Home experience was his attendance at seminary. Like so many of the Mears boys before him at Hollywood Pres., he enrolled at Princeton Theological Seminary, in the fall of 1946. Princeton is the leading graduate school of theology of The United Presbyterian Church in the U.S.A. and has turned out some of the most eminent preachers and Christian theologians of our day. Bill's fondest memories of Princeton Seminary were the occasions he and John MacKay, the school's venerable president at the time, would kneel together for prayer. But Princeton, New Jersey, was far afield from Bright's California Confections in Hollywood (of which he was still president). And it was business responsibilities that forced him to return to Los Angeles the following year.

That was 1947. Fuller Seminary, housed initially in Pasadena's Lake Avenue Congregational Church, had just opened its doors, and Bill became one of its first students, along with Dan Fuller and David Hubbard, now Fuller's president. All three became good friends. Though nondenominational in character, Fuller Seminary has always had strong Presbyterian leanings, and large numbers of its faculty and students have been ordained ministers or lay members of The United Presbyterian Church. Bill stayed at Fuller until 1951; he also remained active in the deputation work at Hollywood Pres. during those years.

VONETTE ZACHARY BRIGHT

The second major event in Bill's life in this period was his marriage. Vonette Zachary had also grown up in Coweta, Oklahoma. Bill was five years older than she, but despite their difference in age, Vonette had watched him closely as they were growing up because, in her words, "Bill was one of the most outstanding young men in our town." His affection for Vonette, however, did not really materialize until he had established his fancy foods business in Los Angeles. During the summer after her freshman year at Texas Women's University, where she graduated with a degree in home economics in 1948, Vonette received a letter from William R. Bright, president of Bright's California Confections, with obvious romantic intent. It took her five and a half months to reply (after all, she hadn't even seen him in two and a half years); but that reply, when it finally came, was the beginning of a regular correspondence—before long they were writing to each other daily. By then, moreover, Bill was well established in his business—definitely on the road to success—and he could afford to send Vonette flowers or candy or telephone her long distance every week. During his first visit to Vonette's campus, he proposed marriage. The engagement was long, however; it lasted for three years.

From the beginning and for some time to follow, there were problems in Vonette and Bill's relationship. Bill had been converted and was attending Hollywood Pres., and although Vonette had always been a churchgoer, it disturbed her greatly when Bill started sending her passages of Scripture to read with his letters and when he began asking her to pray about certain things. Was he some sort of religious fanatic now? That was the big question Vonette asked, and she felt a desperate need to correct Bill's position in order to save their future marriage. As a result, she planned a trip to California, promising her college roommate that she would break the engagement if she couldn't cure Bill of his fanaticism.

Vonette's first acquaintances in Los Angeles were Bill's friends at Hollywood Pres. Showing courtesy, she listened intently to them talk about "what God had done in my life" and "what God showed me in my personal Bible study today." This "testimony English" still bothered Vonette, but she had convinced herself that these people were so excited only because they were new in the faith. It would soon pass—or would it? She was still disturbed, although she had to admit that this was "the sharpest bunch of kooks I've ever seen."

The days passed, and Vonette quickly came to realize that Bill's faith and the faith of his friends were right for *them*. But she also recognized the fact that faith in Jesus Christ meant little to *her*, despite her long-time involvement in the church. Thus she made her decision to stick out the week, then return Bill's engagement ring, after which they would go their separate ways. Vonette still loved Bill dearly, but there seemed to be no other responsible choice she could make.

Bill sensed the dilemma facing his fiancee, and he also knew that unless Vonette shared his faith the marriage couldn't work. So in desperation, he asked her to have a chat with Henrietta Mears, knowing that if anyone were able to change her spiritual disposition, Teacher would be the person. The inevitable happened. After a long period of discussion with Teacher, Vonette did what she thought she had done as a little girl, but what had long since lost its meaning and relevance in her life: She committed herself to Jesus Christ in a personal way and entered the faith Bill had told her about but she hadn't really understood until this moment. The wedding date was set, and Vonette and Bill were married on December 30, 1948, while he was still a student at Fuller Seminary.

Vonette tells that, on their honeymoon, when she was more than willing to fit into Bill's world any way he wished, her husband turned to her and surprised her by saying, "I want you to always be Vonette Zachary. I don't want you to be concerned about 'fitting in' as Mrs. William R. Bright. I married you as Vonette Zachary, and I want you to be Vonette Zachary Bright. Don't try to be anything other than your own person." And to this day, Vonette Zachary Bright *is* her own person. She was co-founder of Campus Crusade for Christ and has always had her own ministry within that organization from its inception. Bill often declares that the three most influential people in his ministry have been women—Mary Lee Rohl Bright, Henrietta Mears, and Vonette Zachary Bright.

2 A Crusader with the Saints

Self-centeredness—Christianity finishes that. How? By taking you, once and for all, right out of yourself. By sending your critical faculty through the baptism of the Holy Spirit of love. By bursting the petty horizons, and shattering the narrow ways, and thrusting you forth, a crusader with the saints, with Christ going on before!

JAMES S. STEWART, *The Gates of New Life*

THE BIRTH OF CAMPUS CRUSADE

Founded as the southern branch of the University of California—which hitherto had only one campus, in Berkeley—UCLA was less than a few decades old when Campus Crusade for Christ was established there in 1951. Today, with close to 30,000 students, the University of California at Los Angeles is located in one of the most fashionable residential and commercial areas in the world—Westwood, California, surrounded by Bel Air, Brentwood, Malibu, Century City, Beverly Hills, and Hollywood. It has become one of America's great universities.

Wednesday-night Bible studies were a highlight in the week for Henrietta Mears' college department at Hollywood Pres., just a few miles from the UCLA campus that many of the students attended. At the conclusion of each meeting, there would naturally follow a "testimony time" (the same thing is now more generally called *sharing*), when students would tell what God had done for them the previous week. It was a good opportunity for fellow students not only to gain inspiration but, more important, to be challenged to do the Lord's work the following week. Of course, Teacher often had bigger ideas and bigger plans than her students, and many times she'd become disgruntled when the testimonies degenerated into petty personal concerns and trivialities. At that point, she would regularly come back with a firm rebuttal, getting the meeting back on track with words like, "This has been the most ridiculous testimony time I think I have ever heard! All we have been talking about is silly little things that don't amount to a hill of beans! Have we lost sight of why we are here? There hasn't been one word about winning the nations for Christ. How about these great campuses in this area? Hasn't anything been done out at UCLA this week? Hasn't anyone witnessed to a student at USC? God weeps over these lost students, and we come here to talk about trifles. St. Paul dreamed about kingdoms brought to Christ. Knox cried, 'Give me Scotland or I die.' Luther wept over Germany."

Among the most active college students at Hollywood Pres., Bill Bright had been leading the church's deputation teams to skid row rescue missions, jails, and hospitals, for years, taking on about thirty deputation assignments per month while he was president of his fancy foods business and a student at Fuller Seminary. "I soon discovered that we had to wait our turn to go to jail services and skid row missions because there were many other churches covering this area of service. One day it occurred to me that there were no waiting lines to reach college students." Bill's words had been preceded by a covenant he and Vonette had drawn up early in 1951 renouncing all of their selfish ambitions and materialism. "On this Sunday afternoon at our home in Hollywood we took a sheet of paper and made a list of all the things we once wanted. We were very ambitious, very determined. Our lists were long. We took them and said to the Lord, we don't want these anymore, we just want to live for you. If you want us to live in a tent, a hole in the ground, or live in some remote part of the world to serve you, we are ready."

The vision for Campus Crusade came to Bill one night while he and Hugh Brom, a close friend at Fuller and now pastor of a Presbyterian church in Glendale, California, were studying for a Greek exam in February, 1951, just as Bill was in his final few months of seminary and Vonette's teaching career was developing: "Suddenly, without any warning, it was as if I was in the very presence of the Lord. The sense of his glory and greatness was overwhelming. There in just a few brief moments it was as if the Lord laid out the broad brush strokes of a great canvas that embraced the whole world. At this time and in a very definite way, God commanded me to invest my life in helping to fulfill the Great Commission in this generation, specifically through winning and discipling the students of the world for Christ. It was an intoxicating experience. I was filled with joy. I remember Hugh looking on in amazement, not knowing exactly what was happening. The experience left me so charged with energy that I asked Hugh if he'd like to take a run with me. So we left our books and took a long run through the Hollywood Hills." Just exactly how Bill and Vonette were to begin this work at UCLA was spelled out to them in the following months as a result of prayer and counsel from friends.

The name *Campus Crusade for Christ* was suggested to Bill by one of his favorite professors at Fuller, Wilbur Smith, who taught English Bible. Although he was very close to graduation, Bill couldn't wait to begin laying the groundwork for his new ministry. Lack of a seminary degree would prevent him from being ordained in The United Presbyterian Church, but he had become convinced that "God did not want me to be ordained. Though I have a great respect and appreciation for clergy, layman status has often worked to a great advantage in my ministry with students and laity." So he left Fuller, sold the fancy foods business, and moved with Vonette to a rented house one block from the UCLA campus. UCLA was a logical choice for Campus Crusade's beginnings. It was close by, and both of them had witnessed there during the previous year. Furthermore, it was a very secular campus, and the denominational ministries serving UCLA at the time were not conducting the kind of vigorous evangelistic outreach Bill and Vonette envisioned. From the start, the Brights held meetings for groups of students in their home, which at first was adjacent to sorority row.

Bill immediately organized a board to advise him on establishing

Campus Crusade. In the beginning, it included as members Henrietta Mears, Billy Graham, Dawson Trotman, Dan Fuller, and J. Edwin Orr, the noted historian of revivals who helped motivate Graham's recommitment to Christ at Forest Home and was chaplain to the Hollywood Christian Group.

Bill and Vonette moved close to campus on October 1, 1951, and were able to start their work and live modestly for the first few years from the sale of Bill's business. Henrietta Mears had always been a firm believer in personal and corporate prayer, and this conviction certainly rubbed off on the Brights, who initiated Campus Crusade at UCLA by organizing a twenty-four-hour prayer chain among church members with the single request that "God would do a unique thing on the UCLA campus." Next they began recruiting students to join them in visiting fraternities and sororities and other living groups. Bill had a specific interest in reaching "Greeks" and athletes at UCLA, because at this time they were the prominent and influential campus leaders who could be most effective in having an impact on other students. Furthermore, in terms of appearance, background, personality, and "style," Vonette and Bill were especially compatible with these particular students.

Within just a few months, more than 250 UCLA students—including the student body president, the editor of the campus newspaper, and a number of top athletes (among them Rafer Johnson, the world decathlon champion)—had committed their lives to Christ. Word traveled quickly, and soon Christian leaders at other campuses began asking the Brights to establish the same kind of movement at their colleges and universities. Bill and Vonette recruited their first full-time staff—six young men who received a salary of $100 per month for only nine months of the year—and by 1952 Campus Crusade had spread to several other campuses, including San Diego State, the University of Southern California, the University of California at Berkeley, and the University of Washington. During 1952–1953, the Brights lived in J. Edwin Orr's home while he traveled, and the movement at UCLA continued to grow rapidly. Like their first home near campus, Orr's residence was also located in Westwood and provided a good atmosphere for the at-home Bible-study and fellowship groups Bill and Vonette regularly hosted in their ministry.

As time went on, however, it soon became apparent that the Brights and their staff needed a permanent base of operation for the work of Campus Crusade at UCLA and elsewhere. Bill relates the outcome of that need: "Day after day, on my way to campus, I passed a large home of Moorish castle style architecture with a 'For Sale' sign on the lawn." The house was situated perfectly for Vonette and Bill's purposes, on the north side of Sunset Boulevard, in Bel Air, but directly across from the UCLA campus. "I had promised Vonette when we were married that one day we would live in Bel Air, so I was tempted again and again to stop and inquire about it."

But the whole issue turned out to be a difficult struggle for Bill. "I rejected the idea as being a personal, selfish desire, until one day I became convinced that perhaps God did want us to acquire this property, inasmuch as it was located only about three minutes from the heart of the UCLA campus." With that, he finally stopped to investigate the home and ask its price. Unfortunately, Bill's money from the sale of his fancy foods business was already tied up in the ministry, and the asking price for 110 Stone Canyon Road was far too much for him to even contemplate at the time. So, he says, "I put the idea out of my mind."

Nevertheless, it wasn't long before Henrietta Mears learned about the Brights' fascination with the Bel Air property. She admitted that she, too, had considered buying the mansion some years previously, but her sister Margaret never shared that interest. Now that Margaret was dead, however, it was getting too difficult for her to live in and maintain their big two-story home, also near the UCLA campus, alone and without help. Thus Teacher decided to purchase the mansion on Stone Canyon Road as her home, with the promise that Bill and Vonette would move in with her, maintain the house, and pay their fair share of the expenses. Laid out in the shape of an *H*, the mansion was huge, and both the Brights and Henrietta Mears had more than enough privacy. It always remained a cooperative venture, however, and the two households and their guests did get together regularly for meals in the enormous dining room.

THE MOVEMENT SPREADS

Campus Crusade for Christ now had its first headquarters, and within days as many as 300 students at a time began pouring in for meetings. The mansion on Stone Canyon Road was more than adequate for the ministry until 1956, when the annual summer task of training their growing staff put Bill and Vonette in an awkward position. More space was needed. It worked out that, during the fall of that year, five acres of choice land on the shores of Lake Minnetonka in Mound, Minnesota, were given to the organization as the site of its new training center. "In the summer of 1957 we completed a beautiful chapel and dormitory combination, which, together with the existing facilities which we had also remodeled, enabled us to train approximately 150 people at a time." By then it was clear to Bill and to others that his original vision was finally beginning to materialize as a reality.

Meanwhile, the movement continued to spread from campus to campus. Many hundreds of students were actively involved in Campus Crusade, the staff was increasing in size, and the training program for staff, still one of the most important facets in the organization's ministry, became more structured and was improved. Campus Crusade's growth would continue, both at UCLA and elsewhere, until 1961, when yet another move would be contemplated, one that would make all of Bill's plans and dreams up until that time seem trivial by comparison.

Arrowhead Springs had been a famous resort in the foothills of Southern California's San Bernardino Mountains at least since 1939, when the present hotel structure of concrete and steel was built, financed by a group of well-to-do Hollywood film stars. Various Indian tribes had come to this spot for centuries, bringing their sick and wounded for healing in the natural hot mineral springs. They called the place holy land, and all weapons of warfare were laid aside here. The first hotel and spa had been constructed on the property in 1854 by David Noble Smith and was widely advertised as a health resort. The original hotel was destroyed by fire, and two others followed. They, too, were razed. The most recent hotel was opened in December 1939, when Rudy Vallee, Al Jolson, and Judy Garland entertained on the first night of its operation. Arrowhead Springs soon became a popular retreat for the movie colony and for top business executives. It was only a short drive from Los Angeles, even before freeways. With the development of better transportation, the stars began traveling farther afield, at least to Palm Springs and Las Vegas, and Arrowhead Springs turned into something like a white elephant. Several different owners had tried hard to restore the property to its original status, to no avail, when Bill Bright first arrived to view the resort in 1961. At that time it consisted of 1,735 acres, with ten private bungalows, dormitory facilities for several hundred, an auditorium built to accommodate 700 people, a recreation house, four tennis courts, a stable, two large swimming pools, and the central 136-room six-story hotel.

By 1960, Campus Crusade's staff numbered 109, and the movement was active on forty campuses in fifteen states. It had a weekly radio broadcast on several stations, and significant work had already been established in South Korea and Pakistan. Once again, Campus Crusade for Christ had outgrown its Westwood headquarters and, now, its Lake Minnetonka training center as well. Another move would have to be undertaken.

It didn't take Bill a long time to decide that Arrowhead Springs would be ideal for the headquarters of Campus Crusade for Christ International, despite its $2 million price tag. Bill says that, while he was praying on the floor of the abandoned hotel that first visit, "God spoke to me as clearly as if there had been a public address system in the room. Unmistakably I heard him say, 'I have been saving this for Campus Crusade for Christ. I want you to have it, and I will supply the funds to pay for it.'" $2 million was, in fact, a bargain for property that had been appraised at $6.7 million, and it was in remarkably good condition, too. But just like 110 Stone Canyon Road, Arrowhead Springs seemed unobtainable. Bill admits that the asking price was "an incredible amount for our organization, which had never had an extra dollar in its ten years of existence." Nevertheless, Vonette and Bill and their staff prayed for fourteen months that the money would eventually become available. "Even though there was no tangible evidence of the fact," Bill related, "I knew that God wanted us to move to Arrowhead Springs."

By this time, Bill and Vonette had attracted the attention of a number of wealthy and prominent businessmen as friends and supporters of the movement. One of these, Henry Hanson, had formulated a proposal for obtaining the hotel. On the basis of loans and gifts, the Campus Crusade for Christ board of directors made an offer of a $15,000 deposit toward the purchase price, with an additional $130,000 to be paid within thirty days after the signing of the contract. It was accepted. With that, the movement's headquarters were moved from Westwood to Arrowhead Springs on December 1, 1962. The initial $130,000 was raised at the last minute, and Bill rushed to San Francisco personally to make the payment and secure the purchase.

The question remained, however, as to how the balance was to be collected. An unusual offer came to Campus Crusade from Guy F. Atkinson, a leading builder of multimillion–dollar construction projects. He proposed giving $300,000 to the organization if the balance of the debt were raised *in toto* within one year from that day. And so the fund raising continued. But on the evening of the deadline, when every conceivable source of revenue had been exhausted (including the sale of some of the land), $33,000 was still needed. During the last few hours before the midnight deadline, Bill made some phone calls to collect a couple of pledges he had forgotten about. The calls were productive, and soon some of the movement's staff who, at the time, hardly had enough to live on themselves, gave additional small amounts of $25 or so. Yet $10,000 was still required. In the last fifteen minutes before midnight, Vonette remembered that $5,000 had been set aside by the organization in case of a special need. A call to the property manager confirmed its availability, and the final $5,000 was promised too. Although that was not the end of the financial trauma for Arrowhead Springs—in fact, difficult land negotiations almost cost the loss of the property just ten days later—$2 million collected in a such a short time had served to authenticate Bill's initial "conversation" with God about the resort only a few years before.

In the first year of Arrowhead Springs as Campus Crusade's headquarters, hundreds of people came there to be trained in evangelism and discipleship. And since then, the Brights' original goal of hosting 1,000 per week at the resort has been exceeded for several months each year, with as many as 1,500 people in attendance for weeks at a time. To the casual onlooker, Campus Crusade occupies the old Arrowhead Springs resort as a result of a combination of good fortune and much determination. But to Bill Bright, it is nothing less than a miracle.

During the 1960s and 1970s, Campus Crusade for Christ as a movement has grown dramatically, and its ministries have been diversified. Major events undertaken by Bill and sponsored by the organization—its milestones—have included a week-long evangelistic "blitz" of the University of California's Berkeley campus in 1967, and in the same city, the quiet founding in 1969 of the Christian World Liberation Front as a radical "front" for Campus Crusade. These preceded two huge evangelistic and training gatherings: Explo '72 brought 80,000 men and women to Dallas, Texas; and Explo '74 attracted more than 300,000 people from eighty-one nations for an international congress on evangelism in Seoul, South Korea, two years later. Also in 1974, the Here's Life, America campaign was launched as an experiment to "saturate" Atlanta, Georgia, with the gospel—utilizing the "I found it!" slogan as an integral part of its strategy. From there, Here's Life spread to selected cities throughout the United States until 1978, when the campaign became international with Here's Life, World. During Christmastime 1977, Bill and Vonette traveled to the Soviet Union for a three-week preaching and evangelistic engagement in Russian Baptist churches. And in the fall of 1978, Campus Crusade's Great Commission School of Theology opened its doors to its first class of seminarians at Arrowhead Springs.

NEW MINISTRIES

The 1960s and 1970s also saw the establishment and further development of new Campus Crusade ministries. In 1963, a young man who had been "discipled" as a student through the campus ministry at Arizona State University asked Bill to be sent forth for Christ as a magician. Today illusionist André Kole spends more than 60 percent of each year on tour, has performed in person in sixty-one nations, and was seen by 78 million viewers on television in 1974. To date he has addressed almost 3,000 separate university and college audiences, and more than 400 copies of his two films are now circulating worldwide.

Another young man who asked Bill for a special ministry in the mid-1960s—this one on the college lecture circuit—is Josh McDowell. McDowell has traveled to almost 550 campuses in over fifty countries in twelve years and has written two best-selling books on Christian apologetics. He is currently also the movement's most visible intellectual.

The Campus Crusade music ministry was founded in 1966; it began modestly with one signing group. Recently, one of the ten groups in the present configuration performed in Malaysia, drawing 18,000 people to two concerts and making them the largest Christian gatherings in that nation in the last 100 years. And in 1969, with less than one complete basketball team, Athletes in Action was formed as Campus Crusade's "ministry to jocks and their fans." Since then, more than 3 million people in live audiences and millions more over radio and television have heard the gospel from the nine AIA teams performing in six sports.

Whereas Bill initiated Here's Life as primarily a ministry of the movement's organized effort to help churches conduct programs in evangelism and discipleship training—its lay ministry—Campus Crusade's *Agape* movement serves as a "Christian peace corps" in many of the world's developing countries, performing what is largely a social ministry there in education, health care, agriculture, and technology.

But the late 1960s also brought two profound changes in the life and work of Campus Crusade for Christ. The first involved the resignation of some of its strongest, most effective, and most prominent staff leaders, leaving Bill Bright as the movement's only major authority figure. The second concerned a pivotal reorganization and "professionalization" of the movement's structure.

THE FAITHFUL MOVE ON

In the late 1960s, Campus Crusade was still mainly a ministry to and with young people. It was therefore only natural that this movement, like the church as a whole, was confronted to one degree or another by the new human concerns and nontraditional lifestyles of the young. The civil rights movement, the antiwar protests, the counterculture, and, later, the Jesus movement all took their toll from the church's leadership and challenged its cherished traditions, which then seemed inextricably bound to what the young activists called "the establishment," both secular and religious. No religious organization appeared more in line with that establishment and its values than Campus Crusade. It was hit hard.

Hal Lindsey had been the popular director of the campus ministry at UCLA. During the beginnings of the Jesus movement, he resigned from Bill's staff to launch a new teaching ministry at UCLA—the Jesus Christ Light and Power Company, more nearly geared to countercultural lifestyles than Campus Crusade had been. "Hal has a particular ministry of prophecy and is a very gifted teacher," explains Bright. "His emphasis at the time was so much on prophecy that we both felt he should have the freedom to teach outside the ministry of Campus Crusade for Christ. I didn't want us to become known as a prophetic movement, and I surely didn't want us to ride any particular theological hobby horse"—a reference to Lindsey's "dispensational" understanding of the Second Coming. Nevertheless, Bill goes on to say, "I still feel very warm affection for Hal." As is well known, Lindsey expanded his nationwide teaching ministry about the Last Days after he left staff, spurred on by the six-day Arab-Israeli war of 1967 (to his mind, a prelude to Armageddon). His Campus Crusade followers then became the first readers of his phenomenally successful bestseller, *The Late Great Planet Earth*, first published in 1970. Those were apocalyptic times, and Lindsey became one of the Jesus movement's leading theoreticians.

Three others who left staff about the same time were Jon Braun, Pete Gillquist, and Dick Ballew. Like Hal Lindsey, all were strong leaders, endowed with much personal charisma. Braun, Campus

Crusade's foremost intellectual at the time, wanted the movement to become a church, in opposition to Bill's conviction that the organization should function rather as a servant of the church. Moreover, Braun began to emphasize, in Bill's opinion, an extreme form of "antinomianism," stressing grace over law in Christian discipleship in reaction to the church's disposition toward legalism in conduct. "The pendulum swung so far that actually some of the young people interpreted Jon's teaching with the exclamation, 'Look, I can do anything I want.' In fact, *whatever* smacked of legalism—like having standards, or training people in a certain structure—was resisted." Bill goes on to explain that "Campus Crusade provides a phenomenal platform, and people applaud and adulate you wherever you go. Because of the availability of this 'instant fame,' Braun and the others may have been victims of their own success, allowing their personal ambitions and ego to get the best of them." But despite the growing rift, Bill had great affection for these comrades-in-arms with whom he'd shared his life and ministry so deeply. "There was real heartache involved. I spent more time on my knees during that period and shed more tears than ever before, because I love these men." Braun, Gillquist, and Ballew resigned in 1968. In 1969, Jack Sparks, one of Bill's chief development officers, with a Ph.D. in statistics from Pennsylvania State University, also forsook Arrowhead Springs—with Bright's blessing—to establish Christian World Liberation Front in Berkeley. 1968-1969 were indeed difficult years for Bill and Vonette. Nevertheless, the movement survived, and more than 500 new staff joined Campus Crusade for Christ during that time.

In the late 1960s, the movement underwent a complete restructuring of the central organization. Years before, Campus Crusade's "paper" advisory board, which included such celebrities as Billy Graham and Senator Mark Hatfield, was disbanded in favor of a "working" board composed of people close at hand—largely business executives—who could meet to set policy more than occasionally. Later, four young men, all working on their M.B.A. degrees at the Harvard Business School, walked into Bill's life. They had been involved with Campus Crusade as college students and were undertaking a movementwide study of the organization as an academic project. The four interviewed more than ninety staff members across the nation and then proposed major structural changes in the movement, changes that freed Bill from the bulk of his administrative duties and greatly reduced the number of staff who reported directly to him. Most important of these men was Steve Douglass, a graduate of MIT as well as of Harvard, who now functions as the organization's vice president for administration.

Reorganization and loss of key personnel in the late 1960s may have transformed Campus Crusade's style as a movement, but it only served to strengthen Bill's original resolve with new strategies to fulfill the Great Commission in this generation.

3 Milestones

Before Christ gave His disciples their Great Commission to begin
that great world conquest which should aim at bringing His
Gospel to every creature, He first revealed Himself in His divine
power as a partner with God Himself, the Almighty One. It was
the faith of this that enabled the disciples to undertake the work
in all simplicity and boldness. They had begun to know Him in
that mighty resurrection power which had conquered sin and
death; there was nothing too great for Him to command or for
them to undertake.

ANDREW MURRAY, *God's Best Secrets*

A milestone can be defined simply as a highly significant point in
development. There have been a number of milestones in the
pilgrimage of Campus Crusade for Christ as a movement. Although
the purchase of Arrowhead Springs itself surely can be described that
way, most of the other events properly termed milestones have been
major gatherings focused on the practice of evangelism.

BLITZ IN BERKELEY

Since the House Un-American Activities Committee hearings led
by Senator Joseph McCarthy in the 1950s, the University of California's Berkeley campus—Cal for short—has been viewed as a hotbed
of political activism, but its strong leftward leanings go back much
farther than that. Furthermore, Cal is certainly one of the greatest
universities in the world. In 1965, the American Council on Education published its first survey, ranking Cal's overall quality of
graduate instruction the best in the country, with Harvard ranked
second. That assessment was reaffirmed in ACE surveys published in
1970 and 1975 as well.

Cal is an enormous state-controlled campus with close to 30,000 students today. It is located in a city where the political conservatives tend to be liberal Democrats and the radicals are orthodox Marxist-Leninists of the Maoist variety—a perhaps unique city inhabited by an incredibly diverse body of students and professors, faithful but burned-out radicals, retired people, far-out freethinkers of various sorts, vegetarians, and the remnant of a beatnik to hippie counterculture that had virtally died out by the mid-1970s. It is also home to hundreds of unemployed academics who can't imagine life anywhere else in "the real world," practitioners of humanistic psychology in its many forms, and devotees of somewhat bizarre and "new" Eastern and Western religious traditions accomodated to the city's distinctive cultural ethos. Just a few "street people" remain in town, standing on Telegraph Avenue on the campus southside or Euclid Avenue directly across the campus northside (the "in" student and faculty residential area). They are unwelcome guests in a city that prides itself on its openness, social concern, and progressive politics.

The Campus Crusade "Berkeley blitz" took place in 1967, only three years after the famous Free Speech Movement of 1964. Although the Cal Campus Crusade chapter had been established in Berkeley since the early 1950s, the blitz was organized specifically to counter the major social and political unrest and turmoil that culminated in the dismissal of Cal's President Clark Kerr. Students and hangers-on were talking about revolution; Campus Crusade talked about another solution, spiritual revolution through Christ. (Incidentally, many of the movement's staff are still unaware that it was the freedom of speech on campus gained by the "radical" Free Speech Movement in 1964 that made its 1967 blitz on campus possible.)

On a wet Saturday afternoon early in the year, 600 students and staff arrived to launch their Campus Crusade national convention in Berkeley. The week-long conclave was planned to draw the diverse delegates into a more effective and unified movement (a real problem at the time) as well as to share the meaning of personal commitment to Christ with campus and community. The big gathering opened on Sunday morning, and at 3:00 in the afternoon 300 Cal athletes and coaches attended a banquet on campus to hear members of Campus Crusade's "jock division" (now Athletes in Action) present their personal testimonies, with Bill Bright as the concluding speaker. Players of almost every varsity sport committed themselves to Christ that week.

Official sessions began on Monday morning and reconvened each morning of the week. There were special meetings for international students in the evenings. Half of all the delegates to this convention were students active in the movement in the United States, Canada, and Latin America. During their spare time, the delegates phoned Cal students who could not be reached by campus group meetings to arrange for personal interviews with them. As the *Daily Californian*, the campus newspaper, reported, "By now, the chances are pretty good that you have been approached at least once by a member of Campus Crusade for Christ."

One day 3,000 jammed the Sproul Hall steps and walkway to hear Jon Braun speak on "Jesus Christ, the World's Greatest Revolutionary." The Forum, then a major coffee house on Telegraph Avenue, was turned over for the whole week to convention delegates, many of whom were assigned to the coffee house to interact with the people there each day and night. Folk music was interspersed with testimonies, including that of Hal Lindsey, the movement's campus ministry director at UCLA at the time. Every night Campus Crusade's singing group, The New Folk, entertained many hundreds at the Berkeley Community Theatre, with Bill Bright, André Kole, and Jon Braun as prominent speakers.

Meetings were held in nearly all the fraternities, sororities, and dormitories. A group then called the University Ambassadors— seventy men and women who eventually started Campus Crusade's European ministry—remained on campus a month longer for follow-up work with new converts, focusing on retreats, Bible studies, and counseling. The convention concluded with a speech by Billy Graham to 300 faculty members and administrators on Friday afternoon and to 8,000 people in the campus Greek Theatre that afternoon. All students who had met Christ during the blitz were contacted again the first week afterward.

Officially, Campus Crusade insists that "hundreds of lives were changed as both students and professors invited Jesus Christ to be their Lord and Savior" during the Berkeley convention. Pete Gillquist suggested soon afterward, "The eyes of the nation, and even the world, have repeatedly turned to Berkeley as the leader in revolutionary thought and action. A spiritual awakening at Cal would make an unprecedented impact on thinking people across the nation."

The Berkeley blitz of 1967 did have an impact. But despite the dedication and loving concern, the "superstraight" appearance and style of the Crusaders on their visit and Billy Graham's messages were not the most effective media for a long-range ministry to the counterculture. A far different approach was needed to have an effective ministry to the counterculture and the radical political community of the young in Berkeley, or elsewhere for that matter. Bill was open to the idea, and two years later, in 1969, that something did happen in the city where radicalism in every form had become a way of life.

CHRISTIAN WORLD LIBERATION FRONT

The Berkeley convention of 1967 had been Campus Crusade's biggest effort at campus saturation evangelism, but Cal and other colleges and universities remained gripped by student turmoil. Riots continued and grew worse, and the counterculture was gaining among the young. Political and social activism was matched by the new religious protests of the Jesus movement, denouncing the religious establishment—the institutional church—for its neglect of the poor and downtrodden, its failure to minister effectively to the young, and, most of all, its *spiritualization* of the demands of Christian love—its seeming refusal to *demonstrate* the love of God to society's dissenters and outcasts. Fanned by increasing opposition to the Vietnam War, racism, poverty, and, more gradually, the oppression of women, from the late 1960s to the early 1970s, the flames of student activism appeared to have become a permanent feature of the U.S. campus scene.

Where would Campus Crusade fit in all this? How could a

straight, middle-class, evangelistic movement "win, build, and send"
men and women among the young if it didn't share their concerns or
even speak their language? These questions were answered when Bill
Bright and a few of his closest colleagues laid the foundation for
Christian World Liberation Front as a Christian counterpart to the
Third World Liberation Front, a Marxist-oriented campus movement active at Cal when CWLF was established there in 1969. Bill
explains: "Christian World Liberation Front was, in the beginning, a
front organization for Campus Crusade. We asked three of our
choicest men to launch it, and most of our staff didn't even know
about the plan. Only about half a dozen of us were aware of what
was happening, and it was a *test*. There was a powerful radical
movement among the students then, and we were trying to figure
out which route to take, whether *we as a movement* should adopt a
radical countercultural approach on campus in order to be all things
to all people that we might win them for Christ. So these men
founded CWLF, and I worked very closely with them."

For people who know Campus Crusade and its style, it is extremely hard to imagine any of its staff fitting into the Berkeley of the late
1960s and early 1970s. It was hard for the three men and their
families to imagine it, too. Jack Sparks, the leader of CWLF,
explains, "Pat grew a moustache and beard for the first time in his
life. Fred's hair grew shaggier (though he never was too particular
about that), and he too had a moustache. Pat's clothes began to
match Fred's in casualness. But the biggest surprise came from me.
The formerly meticulous and suit-clad Jack, I changed dress completely and grew a full beard."

Jack Sparks says, "Obviously there was something significant
behind these superficial changes. They were not undertaken in a
lighthearted fashion or even in a coldly calculated manner. Here
were people with a passionate desire to be God's men and women in
a changing world, and these changes were their immediate adapta-
tions. They were nothing alongside what was to come."

God's Forever Family (CWLF's in-house name) was born in
Berkeley in February 1969 under the leadership of Sparks. At first,
CWLF imitated the political radicals by leafleting their gatherings.

Pat and Fred had been athletes at a large midwestern university, and their conservative backgrounds and associations made it hard for them to see any value in the radicals' critique of the establishment at first. But they did begin to underscore the good on both the establishment side (the Cal administration) and the protestors' side. Soon it became obvious, however, that mere leafleting wasn't enough to make Christ known in Berkeley. Many of the people who read the leaflets—some with Jesus on one side and bail and civil rights information on the other—were homeless, on hard drugs, and physically or mentally ill. Gradually CWLF organized houses with "crash pads" for new converts and other street people to share with their new "family" and growing "beloved community." In July 1969, the first issue of *Right On* (now *Rādix*) appeared—"the underground newspaper from the catacombs of Berkeley"—that provided the first concrete evidence of an effective social action ministry in the Jesus movement, of which CWLF was a leading segment.

As time went on, CWLF itself became radicalized, in a Christian context. Its growing staff, all of whom raised their own support, actually became part of the Berkeley counterculture. The lordship of Christ took on new meanings. Jesus began to be seen as a revolutionary, as exemplified in an early CWLF poster printed in *Right On* and distributed throughout the Jesus movement.

Discipleship also took on a richer meaning. No longer did it have to do only with winning souls and training Christians in the art of traditional evangelism. It also had to do with the new-found costliness of following Jesus, something that was clearly demonstrated to the early CWLF staff as they lived in voluntary poverty with the poor in a city where the church appeared solidly behind the establishment and what CWLF began to view as its un-Christian values.

During this whole time, the Berkeley chapter of Campus Crusade proper continued alongside CWLF, which severed its connection with Campus Crusade only a few months after it started. It has been wrongly assumed that this break was due to CWLF's radicalization and Bill's resulting displeasure. In fact, it was purely a matter of

WANTED:

JESUS CHRIST

ALIAS: THE MESSIAH, SON OF GOD, KING OF KINGS, LORD OF LORDS, PRINCE OF PEACE, ETC.

ALIAS: THE MESSIAH,
SON OF GOD,
KING OF KINGS,
LORD OF LORDS,
PRINCE OF PEACE, ETC.

★ Notorious Leader of an underground liberation movement

★ Wanted for the following charges:

— Practicing medicine, wine-making and food distribution without a license.

— Interfering with businessmen in the Temple.

— Associating with known criminals, radicals, subversives, prostitutes, and street people.

— Claiming to have the authority to make people into God's children.

★ APPEARANCE: Typical hippie type — long hair, beard, robe, sandals, etc.

★ Hangs around slum areas, few rich friends, often sneaks out into the desert.

★ Has a group of disreputable followers, formerly known as "apostles," now called "freemen" (from his saying: "You will know the truth and the Truth will set you free.")

BEWARE — This man is extremely dangerous. His insidiously inflammatory message is particularly dangerous to young people who haven't been taught to ignore him yet. He changes men and claims to set them free.

WARNING: HE IS STILL AT LARGE!

governance. Arrowhead Springs policy dictated that all of CWLF's major plans, and all publications, be approved by headquarters. But time would not allow for this; Berkeley was in crisis, and the only effective ministry to campus and community in these years was a spontaneous ministry, geared to the urgent needs of the moment. Bill understood the situation, and let the founders of CWLF go to minister on their own with his blessing.

CWLF grew throughout the early and mid-1970s to include, in addition to *Right On*, an established crash pad on Dwight Way; a ranch in the country for long-term rehabilitation of troubled youth; a "spiritual counterfeits" project to warn Christians about false cults and messiahs proliferating in an age of new religious and cosmic consciousness; and a house church. In 1975, Jack Sparks joined with some of his former Campus Crusade brothers, including Jon Braun, Pete Gillquist, and Dick Ballew, to form a new, sacramentally "high" church called the New Covenant Apostolic Order, and CWLF changed its name to the Berkeley Christian Coalition.

The counterculture is now virtually dead, though many of its concerns—social justice, the search for community, and personal freedom, among others—have had a great impact on both society as a whole and the church in particular. Witnessing the demise of that counterculture and student activism, Bill Bright and his staff decided against changing the movement's style to parallel that of CWLF. It simply wasn't necessary, even though Bill remains proud of what CWLF has done. Today Berkeley's Campus Crusade chapter is again strong as more traditional values reemerge even in what is affectionally and appropriately termed Berserkeley.

EXPLO '72: ACRES OF CHRISTIANS IN DALLAS

Two major evangelistic gatherings were sponsored by Campus Crusade in the years immediately following the founding of CWLF in Berkeley. Unlike most evangelistic events of this kind, however, both were focused not merely on conversion to Christ but also, if not primarily, on training men and women to *do* the gospel. In the words of Bill Bright, "We were all a part of a gigantic and never-to-be-forgotten demonstration of God's love. Christian joy was in evidence everywhere as tens of thousands of young and not-so-young Christians literally bubbled over like fountains with the love of the Lord."

Dallas, Texas, was the scene of the first major gathering—Explo '72—which took place during the peak of the Jesus movement on June 12–17, 1972. Billy Graham, honorary chairman of the conclave, summarized its intended purpose well:

1. To dramatize the Jesus revolution;
2. To teach youth how to witness for Christ;
3. To remind the church that the old-time Gospel is relevant to this modern generation;
4. To teach young Christians that true faith must be applied to the social problems of the world;
5. To enlist thousands of new recruits for missionary societies, seminaries and Bible schools;
6. To assist the church in evangelism;
7. To evangelize the world in our generation; and
8. To say to the whole world that Christian youth are on the march!

Explo '72 opened officially on Monday, June 12. Scores of buses carrying delegates began arriving at 3 A.M., chartered by 1,300 delegations from 1,000 cities. They sought the sixty-three different locations where specialized training would take place. These buses were joined by chartered jets, cars, and motorcycles. Thousands of Dallasites opened their homes to the overflow who could not be accommodated in Tent City (where 2,000 stayed) or in local hotels and apartment complexes. There were 300 registration, program, and information tables staffed by 2,000 Explo '72 workers on acres of indoor space for foot traffic. This gathering was the culmination of two years' planning and hard work—another one of Bill Bright's impossible dreams.

Explo '72 hired 200 Dallas Transit buses, 750 chartered coaches, and more than 11,000 private autos to transport the delegates to and from the sixty-three conference sites and the Cotton Bowl mass rallies each night. Quantities of food for the 35,000 high schoolers alone were staggering. Dallas food vendors liked to say that the venture of feeding all the crowds must have been without doubt the largest operation of its kind in history.

Explo '72 employed all the new expressions coined by the Jesus movement. It was a reunion of God's Forever Family (not to be confused with CWLF). Training seminars were organized for both high school and college students, business and professional leaders, and lay people in general; in addition to smaller seminars specifically designed for minorities, athletes, internationals, pastors, musicians, and mass media specialists. Campus Crusade reports that Explo '72 drew the largest number of blacks (3,000) and other minorities of any Christian gathering of its kind. In addition to 200 of the movement's staff, 145 other speakers, representing much of the Christian world and all paying their own way to and from Dallas, were involved in the various programs.

Among the tens of thousands of people contacted in homes, apartments, parks, shopping centers, and on streets, more than 10,000 indicated that they had prayed to receive Christ as Savior and Lord. On the final day, 180,000 participants gathered on the edge of the grassy right-of-way near the downtown area where the Woodall Rodgers Freeway would later be built to attend the Saturday "Jesus music" festival. Performers included numerous Jesus rock groups and celebrity vocalists and song writers such as Kris Kristofferson, Rita Coolidge, and June Carter. Johnny Cash introduced Explo '72's last speaker at 2 P.M. that day—Billy Graham, who told those who had come to Christ, "You have a supernatural power to put your hand in the hand of a person of another race. You have a new love in your heart that will drive you to do something about poverty, the ecology question, the racial tension, the family problems and, most of all, to do something about your own life."

Indeed, social concern *was* a theme of Explo '72. It did offer an opportunity for white Campus Crusaders and Jesus People to mix and have fellowship with 3,000 blacks—some of them for the first time. Lectures on "black theology," then relatively new, were popular. Tom Skinner, the one-time Harlem gang leader and now prominent black evangelist, explained to the delegates that black theology is part of black consciousness and, as such, is "simply an attempt to come to grips with what God has to say about black people's struggle and black people's destiny in America."

But there were Christian radicals in attendance who felt strongly that Explo '72 had not done enough to emphasize the social dimension of the gospel. One radical Christian group had made plans to register protests on behalf of their own social and humanitarian causes but backed off when they were allowed to freely distribute their literature. At a large meeting, the Navy chief of chaplains was introduced as a speaker only to be greeted by another Christian group who began chanting antiwar slogans. Upon leaving the platform, this naval officer was met by members of that same group who asked him, "Admiral, can you say you love us now?" Throwing his arms around several of them, he replied, "Yes, I love you." The reply brought tears to many of the demonstrators' eyes, as they threw their arms around him and then followed him to his seat. On Thursday night, Bill Bright told his audience that the "greatest need of the twentieth century is a rediscovery of the revolutionary love of the first century." The Bible "commands us to love God, our neighbors, ourselves, and our enemies." With that, he charged each person there to prepare a list of every person with whom he or she was in disagreement, against whom he or she had a grudge or a "critical spirit." "Then begin to love them by faith. Anyone who is living in love is living in God and he is living in us."

At the end of Explo '72, 80,000 people rose to their feet in practically one accord, responding to the invitation to dedicate themselves to Christ and to the fulfillment of the Great Commission. Numerous local churches had joined together with delegates from 100 countries, many in the Third World, and hundreds of worldwide denominations and organizations to demonstrate to each other a heartfelt sense of Christian love and cooperation that made Explo '72—one of Bill's impossible dreams—a memorable reality for those who were part of it.

EXPLO '74: A MILLION PEOPLE GATHER IN SOUTH KOREA

Plans for a second week-long international evangelistic and training gathering in Seoul, South Korea, were announced in Dallas in 1972. But Explo '74 would attract many more people, far exceeding Bill Bright's fondest hopes.

For a whole year before Explo '74 came to fruition in August 1974, many Christians in South Korea prayed daily for the upcoming congress. At least thirty fasted and prayed for forty days and nights. On August 13, a spontaneous, unscheduled prayer meeting brought together 300,000, a good number of whom remained all night. Hundreds of families tithed their rice to help provide food for the delegates, while twenty college students sold their blood to pay for registration.

Delegates came from every province of South Korea and seventy-eight other countries. Almost all Protestant churches in South Korea, numbering some 12,000 congregations, were represented. According to staff reports, it was the largest Christian gathering in recorded history (at least two of the evening mass rallies exceeded 1.3 million by official police estimate). A total of 323,400 delegates were trained in evangelism and discipleship during one week. Staff members talk about "the largest all-night prayer meetings in the history of the Christian church, and the largest personal witnessing campaign ever conducted (more than 420,000 heard the gospel in one afternoon, and a recorded 274,000 indicated decisions for Christ)."

Approximately 176,000 of those who attended slept on the floor in one of 2,944 primary, middle, and high school classrooms. Another 44,000 chose to live in Tent City on Yoido Island. The delegates all endured two days of rain and sweltering heat when the sun shone each afternoon.

The schedule of events was structured in a manner very similar to Explo '72—training seminars in the morning and mass meetings in the evening, with speakers like Bill Bright; Kyung Chik Han, pastor emeritus of Seoul's Young Nak Church, the world's largest Presbyterian congregation; Samuel Moffett, president of Presbyterian Theological Seminary, Seoul; and Peter Beyerhaus, professor of mission at the University of Tübingen, Germany (and one-time president of its Protestant theological faculty). The gathering itself was spearheaded by Joon Gon Kim, a Fuller Seminary graduate and Campus Crusade's director for South Korea.

Perhaps the most moving part of the gathering was when Akiri Hatori, the noted Japanese evangelist, spoke for the 1,000 Japanese

delegates on South Korea's National Liberation Day, marking freedom from Japanese occupation 29 years earlier. "I stand here with a
broken heart for the sins we Japanese have committed against you.
We ask your forgiveness in Jesus Christ and long to be like you
Christians in Korea, sacrificing ourselves." The impact of that
statement can only be felt if one is aware that Japan and Korea have
always been enemies. When the Japanese forced the Korean people
to worship Shinto gods, many persecutions occurred. Today, 90
percent of all Koreans still have resentment and hatred toward
Japan.

But the success of Explo '74 felt by Campus Crusade staff and the
participants was countered by strong protests by the media and the
movement's critics. Some saw a link between Bill Bright and the
right-wing, anticommunist government of Park Chung Hee, South
Korea's president. It is true that the government did treat Campus
Crusade staff and congress participants well and cooperated with
them fully, but the event was funded totally from the Christian
community. The flames were further fanned when Bill told a
probing reporter, "There is more religious freedom in South Korea
than in the United States," a statement heard around the world. He
also gave the reporter what many critics felt was an inadequate
recognition of the plight of numerous Korean political prisoners—
many of them Christian ministers and lay leaders—who oppose the
policies of the Park regime as contrary to the will of God. One
radical Christian journal in the United States termed Explo '74 an
exercise in "evangelism without the gospel." Other magazines and
newspapers expressed a similar critique. The growing controversy
surrounding Bill Bright continued as Campus Crusade staff and the
participants looked back on Explo '74 as a "miracle among the
masses," which helped in part to spur the growth of the Korean
church from 3 million in 1974 to 7 million in 1978, while critics saw
it as a "big show" at best and an attempt to legitimize and give
credibility to the Park regime at worst.

HERE'S LIFE, AMERICA; HERE'S LIFE, WORLD!

"I found it!" is a slogan well known to most Americans—laughed
at by some (witness the alternative bumper stickers saying "I lost it!"

"I stepped in it!" and—from the Jewish community—"We never lost it!"), criticized seriously by others, and appropriated personally by still others. The slogan itself was coined by Bob Screen of the Russ Reid advertising and public relations agency in Pasadena, California for Campus Crusade's most recent evangelistic outreach, Here's Life, America.

The Here's Life movement was aided considerably in the planning stages by Charles Stanley, pastor of Atlanta's First Baptist Church. Stanley is a very successful parish minister, but he felt strongly that the whole city of Atlanta, with its 1.6 million people, needed to be reached for Christ. He recalls praying, "Lord, there is no way, personally, for me to reach this city. There's just no way to do it. I'm just one man—there are a lot of other churches here and maybe we could somehow all get together." Two Campus Crusade staffers in the city learned of Stanley's concern. They called Bill Bright about it while he and his top associates were planning a pilot saturation evangelism project. The result? Atlanta came to be chosen as a target city number one for Here's Life, America, beginning in 1974.

The movement was to be developed along certain guidelines formulated at the outset. Its focus would be the major metropolitan areas of the United States, where 75 percent of our population reside, and the campaign would be conducted primarily by local churches, assisted by willing pastors, lay leaders, and Campus Crusade staff—who would take on a low profile and act mainly as advisors (many Americans aren't even aware of the organization's involvement in Here's Life). Like other Campus Crusade projects, this movement would concentrate not only on evangelism per se but also on "disciple making." Finally, it was recognized that from the start targeted cities would have to be broken down into regions and neighborhoods and, ultimately, into street blocks of approximately fifty homes each in order to facilitate personal contact between movement workers and those they wished to reach.

Bill judged the Atlanta pilot project a success, and by fall 1977 Here's Life had moved to 200 metropolitan areas in the United States. The strategy in each city was similar. Local churches were methodically invited and encouraged to host or participate in the fourteen-hour planning meetings held before each citywide cam-

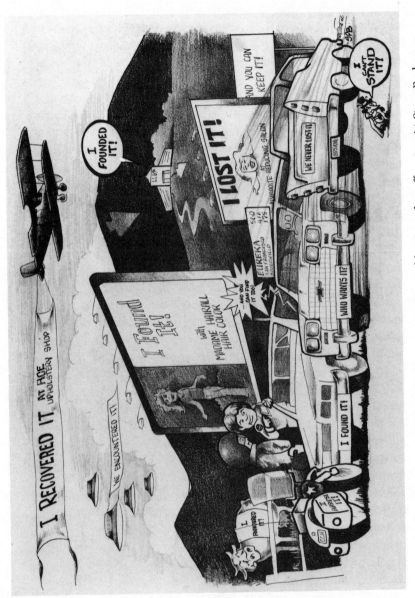

Varied responses to the "I found it!" campaign depicted by Crusade staff cartoonist Steve Becker.

paign. The churches were responsible for the bulk of expenses associated with I found it! though Campus Crusade did provide its development staff to assist local coordinating committees. The total cost of the program itself was more than $8 million, and over 322,000 individuals underwent the extensive training sessions in personal evangelism and discipleship. Interchurch cooperation was indeed impressive.

Action was initiated by organizing a twenty-four-hour prayer chain in each city. Two television specials were put together, featuring such celebrities as Pearl Bailey, Charles Colson, Dean Jones, Roy Rogers, Dale Evans, Pat Boone, and Johnny Mann. Another celebrity, Rosalynn Carter, was part of the Atlanta prayer chain, and she hosted a prayer meeting for 500 in the Georgia governor's mansion. Rosalynn and her husband Jimmy helped launch Atlanta's media campaign with a press conference in the city as well.

Media were an extremely important aspect of Here's Life, America. There were no mass rallies this time. Rather, each targeted city was blitzed with radio, television, and newspaper advertising, billboards, bumper stickers, and lapel buttons. Feature stories on the I found it! campaign appeared in hundreds of major newspapers. The marketing consultants of Campus Crusade estimate that 179 million people (89 percent of the U.S. population) were exposed to the I found it! commercials and television specials. Telephone numbers were listed with the advertising, and two million incoming calls were received in 217 telephone centers, with more than 800,000 individuals requesting copies of the I found it! booklet. In addition, many millions of phone calls went out from those centers at the staff workers' initiative. All in all, more than half a million decisions for Christ were recorded, with many more never making it on to the tally sheets.

In January 1977, Phase II of Here's Life, America was introduced at Arrowhead Springs to encourage ongoing training programs in evangelism and discipleship, again geared to the ministry of local churches; to motivate continuing citywide prayer efforts; increase the vision of lay people to reach other cities, rural areas, and countries with the I found it! strategy; and sponsor momentum-building events that would act as evangelistic catalysts. Phase III planning calls for an expanding emphasis on discipleship and evangelism through the local church, including the use of mass media. In 1977, Here's Life, World was launched to take the I found it! strategy started in the United States to at least 100 new countries on every continent.

Bill Bright insists that Here's Life as a whole has been a phenomenal evangelistic success and that its continuing programs in discipleship training promise Christian growth for both individual participants and their churches. But, like other Campus Crusade projects, this one has received its share of criticism. Church growth specialists have concluded, as a result of their surveys, that, by and large, churches have reaped very few new members because of Here's Life. Bill answers the finding by citing Billy Graham's statement that the success of *his* crusades cannot be adequately determined for at least five years after their conclusion. He also argues that the widespread availability of popular religious television programming keeps many Christians out of church. Others have criticized what they see as a shallow, superficial, and too businesslike evangelistic approach in the Here's Life strategy. Still others, radical Christians especially, question the whole concept of conversion, salvation, and discipleship espoused by the movement as simplistic and focused far too much on the personal spiritual life to the neglect of the social dimension of the gospel. And the debate continues.

PREACHING IN THE SOVIET UNION

The next milestone in the life of Campus Crusade for Christ differs considerably from the others in style though not in purpose. At the invitation of church leaders representing the All-Union Council of Evangelical Christians-Baptists of the U.S.S.R., Bill and Vonette Bright and their party traveled to the Soviet Union for a three-week speaking tour from December 20, 1977 to January 10, 1978. Bill preached fifteen times in seven cities, including Moscow, Leningrad, Kiev, Minsk, and Tula. Approximately 15,000 people attended these meetings, with services that generally lasted three or four hours each and concluded with an invitation for individuals to publicly receive Jesus Christ as their Savior and Lord.

It must be pointed out that, in the Soviet Union, religious freedom is guaranteed by the new constitution, but it is seen in a different light by the government than by outsiders. Soviet Christians may freely worship in their prayer houses, but public proclamation or private sharing of the gospel by citizens is not allowed in certain areas of the country. Furthermore, atheism is a requirement for membership in the Communist Party, and only party members are permitted to serve in leadership positions in the Soviet Union.

Wherever Bill spoke, the churches were filled to capacity and more. He preached to 1,800 at the First Baptist Church of Moscow. On Christmas Day, Bill spoke at two special services held at the Leningrad Baptist Church, together lasting a total of seven hours. Although the church seats only 600 people, more than 2,000 crowded in for each service. "Each time we left a church, the Christians sang 'Blest Be the Tie that Binds' or 'God Be With You 'Til We Meet Again,' and they waved their handkerchiefs. It was always a deeply moving experience to sense that we were now truly wed together in the love of Christ even though we had never met before." Before leaving, Bill offered to supply 1 million Bibles to the Soviet people. No commitments were made by government officials, but Bright remains hopeful that his offer will eventually be accepted.

Unlike previous milestones in the history of the movement, Bill and Vonette's three-week visit to the U.S.S.R. received very little press coverage. Given Bill's politically conservative reputation in the world media, it is somewhat surprising that the Soviet government even issued visas to the Brights and their party, especially for an explicitly evangelistic tour. However, not only the party was welcomed by the Baptists, it was also received at the University of Moscow and by the Peace Committee and the Council of Ministers on Religious Affairs in the U.S.S.R.

Critics who have followed Bill's public remarks for years, including those he made at the conclusion of Explo '74, may be amazed at what the president of Campus Crusade said at a news conference on January 6, 1978, in Moscow. It sums up his experience in the Soviet

Union well, but it also displays a positive attitude on Bill's part
toward peaceful intergovernmental relations, even between capitalist
and communist countries, that the press rarely picks up. In answer to
a reporter's question, "While visiting the Baptist churches and the
Christian people here, did you hear of any limitations in freedom of
worship?" Bill replied by saying, "I have heard rumors of persecution and discrimination, but I am in no position to make a judgment.
I think many of the criticisms that are often made concerning a lack
of religious freedom are without basis in fact. Of those I have been
able to check out, I have been encouraged to believe that there is a
growing opportunity for Christians to worship. One of my reasons
for coming at the gracious invitation of the Baptist Union was to help
build bridges of love and trust between believers in the United States
and the Soviet Union and between our governments, as well as all
nations. I have been encouraged by what I've seen."

THE SCHOOL OF THEOLOGY OF THE INTERNATIONAL CHRISTIAN GRADUATE UNIVERSITY

The most recent milestone in Bill Bright's ministry and in the work
of his movement is The School of Theology of the International
Christian Graduate University, the first component of what Bill
hopes will be a major graduate level university. The seminary
opened its doors to students for the first time in the fall of 1978.

Early in the history of Campus Crusade, Bill tried hard to recruit
staff who were both college and seminary graduates, individuals
having at least seven years of higher education in their backgrounds.
But very few interested seminary graduates could be found. After
that much costly education, most graduates preferred taking on a
parish ministry or denominationally supported campus ministry with
its relative financial security to raising support for themselves and
their families in order to join Campus Crusade's staff. Thus it
became necessary for Bill to modify the movement's original requirements, allowing him to recruit college or university graduates
without a formal theological education, and such people represent
the vast majority of staff today. Although each staff person must

attend Campus Crusade's training programs, which include basic theological education, every year, the depth of this preparation simply hasn't been enough to meet the goals of the movement.

Begun at Arrowhead Springs headquarters, the School of Theology is open to present and future Campus Crusade staff and to others preparing for a variety of ministries, among them the parish. It intends to offer the standard M.Div. degree, the first professional degree in theology, usually required for ordination, as well as several M.A. degrees in specialized disciplines. In addition, the school has several characteristics that make it different from other graduate schools of theology. One is its development of team ministries for husbands and wives. From the start, Campus Crusade has insisted that married people cannot be hired unless both spouses are willing to join staff together; therefore, the school accepts married students as a team. The new seminary will follow a unique curriculum, developed on a cross-cultural basis that utilizes theological and training materials from Latin America, Africa, and Asia, as well as Europe and the United States. What is particularly novel about this curriculum, however, is that at least half the students' time will be spent in practical training for ministry. Moreover, regular faculty will also be required to work and minister *with* their students in evangelism and discipleship as examples of what they are teaching.

Few, if any, Protestant or Catholic seminaries in the United States have solved the very real problem of effectively integrating theoretical, highly academic theological education with meaningful and challenging practical experience in ministry (fieldwork). If the Great Commission School of Theology succeeds here, it is certain that many other schools of theology will have to take a hard look at what it's doing.

PART II
COMMUNITY

4 Winning, Building, Sending: Campus Crusade Inside Out

> In the world the Christians are a colony of the true home, they are strangers and aliens in a foreign land, enjoying the hospitality of that land, obeying its laws and honoring its government. They receive with gratitude the requirements of their bodily life, and in all things prove themselves honest, just, chaste, gentle, peaceable, and ready to serve. They show the love of God to all men, "but specially to them that are of the household of faith" (Galatians 6:10; II Peter 1:7). They are patient and cheerful in suffering, and they glory in tribulation. . . . But they are only passing through the country. At any moment they may receive the signal to move on. Then they will strike tents, leaving behind them all their worldly friends and connections, and following only the voice of their Lord who calls. They leave the land of their exile, and start their homeward trek to heaven.
>
> DIETRICH BONHOEFFER, *The Cost of Discipleship*

PERSONNEL: WHO THEY ARE, WHY THEY SERVE, WHEN THEY LEAVE

"We see our work as a way of life—not as a job. If you don't care what you have or don't have, you'll never be hurt. Give all that you are and have to the Lord. You don't need to be protective of your time, talent, or treasure. They all belong to him. *We don't look for comfort, we give up our rights.* There will always be too much to do, there will never be enough time, enough money, or enough staff to get the job done. This is where God wants us to be. All of the resources belong to the Lord anyway. God can still do it some way. Just be faithful." These words from the Campus Crusade campus

ministry manual aptly describe what it takes to be an effective and happy staff member of the movement. Indeed, those staff who really take this advice seriously and without reservation are the ones who "succeed" in the ministry of Campus Crusade for Christ.

Individuals come to join the movement as a vocation from many different backgrounds and for just as many reasons. In general, a college or university bachelor's degree is a necessary requirement, but on-the-job training is often sufficient experience for those skilled as electricians, printers, plumbers, musicians, secretaries, and the like. On staff there are those with no more than a high school education, and there are Ph.D.s. In the United States, most are white, young, and middle class in background and orientation, though the recruitment of "ethnics" has become something of a priority in recent years.

The campus ministry is still the heart of the movement, and most of the U.S. staff had some prior involvement with Campus Crusade as undergraduates. Campus ministry staff are urged to set a goal of having 40 percent of their "discipled" students go into full-time Christian service (e.g., Campus Crusade staff or seminary). The majority of all staff come from a church background and have been a part of the movement from one to three years, usually as student leaders in a campus chapter. Most are between twenty-five and twenty-nine years of age.

The basic requirements of applicants to the Campus Crusade ministry are simple—"a heart for God and a teachable attitude." Staff standards include spiritual maturity, a calling to the ministry, effectiveness of witness, knowledge of Scripture, an attractive personality, good character, leadership potential, emotional stability, sufficient academic training, a pleasing personal appearance, and requisite physical qualifications. Prospective staff fill out a standard application form and personality questionnaires. References are contacted, and an official staff interview concludes the initial process. All applicants must affirm the movement's seventeen-point statement of faith and its strong emphasis on the infallibility of Scripture as the word of God written. If applicants are married, husband and wife must both apply. Upon acceptance, applicants must attend a four-week Institute of Biblical Studies, followed by a new staff training conference, during which they may indicate their preference for ministry, specific assignment, and location; but applicants are expected to accept the final decision of the personnel office, whatever that might be. When all of this has transpired, each new staff person must raise his or her own support from churches and other organizations and from individuals. Contributors may deduct their support of a staff member from their taxable income, as payment is made to Campus Crusade for Christ directly, after which it is channeled to the designated person or persons.

For beginning staff members, $460 per month is the salary to be raised by a single person, $771 per month by a married couple, plus an additional 17 percent to cover insurance, pension, and overhead expenses. An amount from $127 to $287 per month is to be raised for each dependent child, according to age. All honoraria given to staff are turned over to Campus Crusade, and advancement within the ranks of the organization—attaining a higher staff position—is not rewarded by additional pay. Furthermore, staff may not solicit personal gifts of any kind, although they may accept unsolicited gifts of food, clothing, and other items.

It should be obvious at this point that no one can become wealthy as a regular staff member of Campus Crusade for Christ. Individuals join the movement as a vocation for other reasons. First and foremost, they join because they want to spend their lives sharing their faith with others in order to change the world for Christ. Another powerful motivation has to do with "community." Many staff were so impressed by the community of love and fellowship they found in their Campus Crusade group in college that it seemed only natural to continue that kind of involvement professionally after graduation. For these people, the "beloved community" was so wonderful that nothing could be more rewarding for them than to reproduce that community elsewhere. A large number of people join staff simply because of the encouragement of those already involved. This encouragement by itself guarantees a large applicant pool year after year—a form of "spiritual multiplication," as some Campus Crusaders like to call it. Finally, there are some individuals who have a particular ministry interest that they see best fulfilled in Campus Crusade, which does have a variety of ministries hard to find elsewhere in the institutional church or in other religious organizations.

The worldwide movement now has over 6,500 staff (including "associate staff," who have another job and "donate" their time to Campus Crusade) in ninety-seven countries. Applicants are asked to serve a minimum of two years but are encouraged to make their work in the movement a lifetime career. However, the average length of service of all those leaving the movement is currently only 3.76 years. (This figure does not include the length of service of those still in the movement. If this were to be included, the overall tenure average would be much higher.) Thus the movement, in many ways, is most suitable for people in transition, and it does help them make that transition in responsible ways, giving them the much needed support in choosing a life work that family, friends, and faculty may have been unable to provide.

Why do staff members leave? In assessing the exit interviews of staff, Campus Crusade's personnel office suggests five major reasons: About 23 percent quit in order to get "a change of pace"; 19 percent want a pastorate; 18 percent leave because their spouses have "another call"; 11 percent marry a nonstaff person who doesn't want to join; 6 percent receive placement elsewhere; 10 percent quit without knowing what they'll do next; and the rest have other reasons. What do these people actually do when they leave staff? According to personnel surveys, 29 percent enter secular employment; 21 percent become housewives; 16 percent go on to seminary; 15 percent enter the pastorate immediately; and 9 percent go into another form of Christian ministry.

Behind all these statistics, of course, are reasons for staff exits that never get into personnel files. First of all, many former staff members simply could no longer take the intensity of involvement demanded by the movement. They were physically and emotionally drained and needed a change. Too much work, too little pay, too few rewards. The average pastoral ministry or denominationally supported campus ministry requires less time and offers better pay, which is why Campus Crusade has attracted few seminary graduates to its ministries. Another major reason for leaving staff is that many individuals simply experience a change of perspective while serving in the movement. One ex-staff person, now a doctoral student in New Testament at Harvard, puts it this way: "I began as a student by swallowing the whole thing and marching to the tune as directed. I did not leave the organization with bitterness. My wife and I both felt that we had passed through a stage which was necessary for us because of the background from which we had come." A good number of people join staff from very narrow and parochial religious backgrounds. Campus Crusade broadens their horizons, and they become aware, often for the first time, that the Christian world is much bigger and broader than they had supposed. After awhile, however, Campus Crusade itself becomes too confining for them. They begin to ask questions about the movement and its goals but do not receive what they feel are satisfactory answers. So they move on—some to other religious organizations, some to seminary—in search of greener pastures.

Finally, there are those who leave staff for theological and cultural reasons. They are no longer comfortable in this straight, middle-class movement with its highly developed authority structure, its chain of command, that requires much personal discipline and does not allow its staff to take a public stand on controversial issues or become actively involved in politics. Quite often, these same people wish to change their lifestyles. Some of them joined Campus Crusade to help change the world but found through experience that the movement's ideas about how that should be done—through evangelism and discipleship—did not conform to their own.

Bill Bright is not overly concerned about the high number of staff exits each year. He has always affirmed those Christian leaders and movements that had their spiritual origins in Campus Crusade but moved on to develop their ministries elsewhere. Indeed, it can be argued that the movement's greatest contribution to the church has been the large number of former staff who have become leaders in other spiritual and human endeavors, some of which Campus Crusade could or would not undertake itself.

STAFF TRAINING: DISCIPLESHIP, DISCIPLING, DISCIPLINE

The English words *discipleship, discipling,* and *discipline* all derive from the Latin *discipulus,* a pupil or apprentice, and *disciplina,* meaning teaching or an ordered way of life. Discipleship as a biblical concept is central to the life and work of Campus Crusade for Christ. Within the movement, discipleship is focused on training and teaching in the "school of life," which, for the committed staff member, is itself centered on three activities of ministry: (1) "winning" people—exposing them continually with the gospel through word and deed, with the goal of winning the maximum number to Christ; (2) "building" people—the process of discipling them by offering instruction in the faith, and supportive fellowship, so that they, too, will become disciples ("committed multipliers"); and (3) "sending" people—the natural result of winning and building, whereby discipled Christians will want to be sent out as multipliers to win, build, and send yet others. To quote from the campus ministry manual, "Every ministering activity of every trained Christian should contribute to either winning, building, or sending."

Staff training in Campus Crusade is training in winning, building, and sending people into the world—to help *change* the world—for Christ. It officially begins for a new staff person when he or she attends a four-week Institute of Biblical Studies (held in various parts of the United Sates in summer and winter) that focuses on the study and practical application of Scripture and Christian doctrine. IBS instructors are generally seminary professors, prominent pastors, and senior Campus Crusade staff, whose goal is to build in their students "godly character and the ability to reproduce the likeness of Christ in others." This experience is followed by a period of staff training at Arrowhead Springs in the practical concerns of vocation and ministry. Each year thereafter, the new staff person joins 3,000 other American movement personnel and their trainers, with Bill and Vonette Bright, at Colorado State University, Ft. Collins, for IBS and further practical training in ministry, an ongoing process. Overseas and Latin American divisions of Campus Crusade have their own equivalent training sessions in suitable locations.

The life of a movement staff person is committed to witnessing to his or her faith in Christ, then following up individuals who receive Christ (i.e., introducing them to the "basics" of the Christian faith and life), and, finally, discipling some of them, individually or in a small group (Jesus himself was committed primarily to "the twelve" not to a mass of people). Campus Crusade staffers select to disciple from those they initially follow up people who "seem hungry to know more, read material given them, are willing and eager to meet with the trainer personally or in a group, understand clearly that they have received Christ, ask questions, and respond to the parable of the sower (Mark 4) by wanting to be 'good soil.' " Forty percent or more of a staff member's time may be spent in discipling those chosen individuals.

To the outsider, all of this teaching and training activity may appear as a simple process of ministry. But for the movement's staff, it is a much deeper discipline by which the beloved community is both formed and reproduced. Indeed, the most satisfactory way to understand Campus Crusade for Christ is to see it not merely as a movement but rather as an extended *family*. Entrance into the family is through the discipling experience. Disciples are faithful men and women who are to be treated in a special way by their trainers. As the campus ministry manual puts it: "These faithful men and women will obviously be involved in the total ministry. . . . You will want to pour your life into these few faithful men and women so as to perpetuate 'God's method,' which is men and women. Remember, like begets like. They will normally become the kind of disciple you are. Your goal should be to disciple them to Jesus Christ and not train them to be followers of you or your personality." A student or other person discipled within the movement joins the family "officially," and enters its deepest fellowship, by joining staff.

To be sure, a profound sense of spiritual kinship results between discipler and disciple. The former becomes a spiritual "parent" to the latter, even though the object of the new disciple is Christ not the trainer. (Nothing is more hurtful to a trainer than to see a spiritual "child" depart from the faith or become a backslider.) In many ways, Bill and Vonette, whose relationship is itself viewed as a model

for staff couples and is often emulated by them, function as the
movement's original spiritual parents. They started the family in the
first place (and even lived with a number of their staff in the early
days) by winning, building, and sending—and reproducing in kind.
One can easily look at the annual staff training and IBS gatherings as
a family reunion and as an opportunity to welcome new members
into the family. Finally, staff members relate to each other as
"brother" (less frequently as "sister," however), a designation reserved for fellow believers alone and given their deepest meaning in
reference to the Campus Crusade family.

The higher up one goes in the movement, the more seriously the
discipling process seems to be taken. At the top, the "inner circle"—
now called the president's cabinet—we see the people Bill Bright
pours his life into personally. Their relationship as brothers under the
authority of father is so close and heartfelt that the departure from
staff of any one of them can become an almost unbearable experience for Bill. It is with this understanding of Campus Crusade as a
family that the movement's structure, organization, and chain of
command begin to make sense.

HEADQUARTERS: LIFE AT THE TOP

The core of the Campus Crusade extended family is centered at
the movement's international headquarters at Arrowhead Springs.
Policy is conceived by Bill Bright and his closest advisers, set and
confirmed by a board of directors, and carried out by the organization's staff, who operate within a network of clearly defined roles
and responsibilities. Each member of the family is responsible to his
or her "director," all the way to president's cabinet, the members of
which are responsible to Bill himself.

The board oversees an annual budget—almost $42 million in
1977—of which 66 percent is designated for staff support, 12 percent
for special projects, 8 percent for fund-raising efforts, 7 percent for
central administrative support for ministry programs, and the rest for
miscellaneous expenses. The 1977 budget represented an increase of
22 percent over 1976, and this is in addition to $5 million raised by

the Campus Crusade affiliated ministries around the world. The movement does have *some* very wealthy contributors, but the average gift received by the organization is only $34. In other words extremely large donations are very rare.

Members of the board of directors—a working board—include Bill and Vonette Bright; S. Elliot Belcher, chairman of Southern United Life Insurance Company, Montgomery, Alabama; Bruce A. Bunner, partner of Peat, Marwick, Mitchell & Co., Los Angeles; Arthur S. De Moss, president of National Liberty Corporation, Valley Forge, Pennsylvania; Edward L. Johnson, chairman and president of Financial Federation, Inc., Los Angeles; L. Allen Morris, president of The Allen Morris Company, Miami, Florida; and Arlis Priest, president of Priest Enterprises, Phoenix, Arizona. With the exception of Bill and Vonette, all are successful businessmen in their own right.

Steve Douglass, the principal reorganizer of the movement in the late 1960s and early 1970s, is vice president for administration. In the words of one of his discerning colleagues, he is "tall, business-like, looks like he was born in a gray flannel suit. Soft-spoken, warm personality, with an understated sense of humor. Very sharp, and doesn't feel he has to prove it. Represents the constant voice of reason." Douglass presides over the activities of 750 staff members at international headquarters who provide materials and services to help make other staff ministries more effective.

At Arrowhead Springs are located the president's office and his personal staff; the international ministries office, donor relations office, and *Agape* movement office; computer services, which keep track of an average of 3,500 contributions that come in daily; a mass media department, including publications office, print shop, and creative studios, which develops full-scale public relations and advertising campaigns; audiovisual office; marketing and sales services (2,500 Christian bookstores in the United States carry Campus Crusade publications); and a legal office that fulfills all the functions of a corporate law office and researches court cases pertaining to religious freedom in the United States.

In addition, international headquarters houses the movement's mail systems, handling 6,000 pieces of mail coming in daily; accounting office; personnel department; U.S. field offices, including campus, high school, lay, military, prison, intercultural, and special ministries; conference services; the North American training office; and a word-processing center that types all of Bill Bright's correspondence, receives dictation by phone onto cassette tapes ready for transcription, and types original copies of large quantities of material that would be impossible for office secretaries to accomplish on their typewriters.

Life at headquarters is "life at the top" of the movement. Although only a few Campus Crusade staff members actually live at Arrowhead Springs—Bill and Vonette among them—headquarters staff call themselves a family. New staff begin their ministry at international headquarters with eleven weeks of intensive evangelism and discipleship training on local college and high school campuses and in lay communities (not even headquarters staff are exempt from this responsibility). All the recreational facilities at Arrowhead Springs, such as pool and tennis courts, are, of course, open to staff use. "During our weekly 'Family Devotions,' we pray and sing together and hear speakers and groups from all over the world. Twice each week staff meet within their offices for devotions." So goes the description of the situation in a staff recruitment brochure. These comments attest to a major effort among top Campus Crusade administrators to keep the spiritual life an integral part of daily office routine. Because work in the movement is a way of life and not just a job, headquarters staff do not allow bureaucratization to lead to secularization, as it does in many other religious organizations. Each staff person at Arrowhead Springs—from the "lowliest" janitor to the president himself—has a ministry. And the work is hard, very hard, for everybody.

Like any other similar organization, Campus Crusade has its hierarchy. Top officials have nicer offices (though even Bill's office is nothing to brag about) and eat excellent meals in a special staff dining room in the hotel. The standard mode of dress for movement "executives" at headquarters is coat and tie for men and dresses for women. There is even a staff hair stylist in the hotel for both women and men, but no chauffeur-driven limousines and no cocktail lounge.

The "prime movers" in the U.S. operations at headquarters are the president's cabinet, which consists of seven men in addition to Bill and Vonette Bright. More so even than the board itself, these individuals together represent the heart as well as the brains of the movement. They are Bill's faithful disciples, who report directly to him and are distinguished by two necessary qualifications for the position. First and foremost, these men and one woman are one with Bill's vision. They share it without reservation. Second, cabinet members are loyal to Bill to such a degree that he can trust them without question. Not all are based at Arrowhead Springs, but their spirit pervades the place, and they are held in high esteem by all staff members who know them.

THE ORGANIZATION AND THE MOVEMENT:
STEREOTYPE AND REALITY

A stereotype is a standardized mental picture held in common by a group of people and representing an oversimplified opinion or uncritical judgment of a person, an issue, an event, or a movement. From its inception in 1951, Campus Crusade for Christ has been stereotyped by outsiders—Christians and non-Christians alike—as a movement of superficial cultural and social conservatives wedded to the American way of life and concerned only about people's "spiritual" welfare not about their day-to-day life in the world. They tend to view Campus Crusaders as upstanding, middle-class, moralistic evangelists with one-track minds geared exclusively to "getting people saved" for the next world while they go to hell in this one.

To a point, the stereotype often holds true. The movement's campus ministry manual does go to great lengths about what constitutes proper dress and etiquette for staff members. Detailed instructions are included, for example, on how to escort a woman properly, how to get in and out of a car gracefully, and how to buy clothes wisely. The manual covers appropriate dress for both men and women. For example: "The clothes of a gentleman are always conservative; and it is safe to avoid everything that comes under the heading of novelty. . . . Best dressed men do not wear brown shoes

with blue or gray suits. Even 'cordovan' is not in best taste." And for
women: "Always wear gloves with a hat. . . . White gloves can be
worn with almost anything. They are always proper and can easily
be kept sparkling clean." "Quality brands" of clothes are recommended for both men and women. Specific advice is given on how to
care for clothes and exactly how to wear them. As well as on
grooming and personal hygiene. Women are encouraged to "sit
comfortably and gracefully." They should "walk gracefully" too.
"Walk tall. Feel tall." No rowdy behavior for men. And so on and so
forth until every conceivable social courtesy and pleasantry has been
dealt with. Amy Vanderbilt would be proud of her Campus Crusade
emulators.

Are Campus Crusaders really middle-class in their orientation and
basic values. Yes, indeed, just like most other Americans. And
moralistic, too? Only if that means that they are characterized by a
deep concern for morality, but not a narrow, legalistic concern. Staff
members do hold to a high standard of personal and interpersonal
ethics, grounded in Scripture. And what about those ever-present
smiles? Most photos of Campus Crusade types—including those
featured on the I found it! billboards—show them smiling. In a world
marked more by suffering and oppression than fulfillment, happy
people are often viewed with suspicion. Critics term Campus Crusaders' smiling faces plastic—unreal, inauthentic. How could anyone
possibly be that happy, all the time? This forces us to go beyond the
stereotype, and its one-level truth, to the deeper reality behind it.

True, Campus Crusade staff members do try to dress and behave
like everyone else—the best of everyone else—in the proper cultural
context. The reason for this effort, moreover, is to be "all things to all
people" to win them for Christ. They are surely correct in believing
that most Americans *are* impressed by and will listen to a person
conservatively dressed, well-mannered, and well-groomed by white,
middle-class standards. But where the cultural ethos is different,
where other styles of life predominate, Campus Crusade changes its
emphases in these areas to conform with what is expected. There are
staff people, for instance, who work in ethnic communities in the

United States, in the black and Latino districts of New York, Chicago, and Los Angeles, for instance. The campus ministry manual makes it very clear how white, middle-class staffers are to act in these situations with racial and ethnic minorities: "Be interested in what they feel is important in their culture. Gain appreciation and knowledge of their art and music. Be sensitive to proper clothing to wear. Balance it. Use their system of time. Use their system of space. Make a friend in that culture who will be willing to serve as your 'cultural guide.' Have a mental attitude of being willing to be all things to all people."

Contrary to common belief, Campus Crusade is not trying to bring white, middle-class Christianity to ethnic cultures in the United States. Black staff members are just as black as their sisters and brothers outside the movement, and white staff in the black community are required to make the necessary cultural adjustments for a truly black ministry in that place. Overseas the same thing applies. Most Americans seeking to serve with Campus Crusade anywhere outside the United States must spend fourteen weeks of cross-cultural training in South Central Los Angeles and Watts, living with a black family and attending a black church.

The stereotype of Campus Crusade for Christ as a movement unconcerned about real human needs persists largely because the critics don't *know* its staff. In many cases, they've never even met. It is easy to pass these people off as religious kooks with a superficial, unworkable theology when you don't know them. But when you do get to know them, it readily becomes apparent that their "one-track mind" *is* focused on obedience to Jesus Christ and his will. Eternity is important; but so is time—the here and now—which explains the movement's clear stress on discipleship. Furthermore, staff members are always more than delighted to demonstrate to doubters that their faith does work. Campus Crusade staff have sacrificed a great deal of their treasure, time, and talent to serve in the movement, a fact rarely appreciated by outsiders. They do have "a heart for God and a teachable attitude." If they didn't, they wouldn't be on staff. And the smiles are genuine too. They are, in fact, an open invitation to "get to know us personally. Share in our love for Christ, for each other, and the world." Critics who take the time to get to know these people will, inevitably, be in for some major surprises.

WHETHER WE LIVE OR DIE

Nevertheless, it *is* true that "the world" will always have a difficult time understanding Campus Crusade's one-track mind— that Christ is the center, the final goal of both ministry and life itself and that everything else in a person's life must be subordinate to Christ and his will. On the night of July 31, 1976, Bill Bright received a phone call from Vonette, who was leading a retreat for thirty-five staff women at a ranch some distance from Ft. Collins, Colorado, where summer staff training was about to begin. The Big Thompson River was rising, and she told Bill that the group of them would have to stay put until the waters subsided rather than make the trip to Ft. Collins that evening as originally planned. Bill recounts the incident: "Seconds after she hung up, the lines went dead—a wall of water fourteen feet high was crashing down the canyon where the ranch was nestled. For the next fourteen hours, not knowing where she was or if she and the others were still alive, I relived the twenty-eight joyous and adventurous years of marriage I had shared with the most wonderful person in all the world. Yet during those hours of uncertainty, I experienced personally the peace of God which truly passes all understanding."

Within just a few hours, news came to Ft. Collins of the rescue of two of the women caught in the Big Thompson flash flood, but there still seemed to be little hope for the rest, Vonette among them. "The next day had already been set aside for prayer and fasting as the first day of our staff training," Bill explains. "I told our staff what had happened and encouraged them to join me in praising and thanking God. The Bible tells us 'without faith it is impossible to please God.' The best way I know to demonstrate faith is to praise God, even when our entire world crumbles. So the 3,000 of us praised and thanked him, even as we faced tragedy. . . ." And tragedy it was. In the end, Vonette and most of the other women survived. But seven of them had been identified among the flood victims.

The one-track mind of Campus Crusade is epitomized by what came next. Was it possible that this tragedy could itself be a way to win others for Christ? "These women lost their lives in the Colorado flood. . . . But they are still alive. They have a message for you." That was the opening line of a full-page evangelistic memorial advertisement placed in 8,500 newspapers by Campus Crusade after the catastrophe. "A tragedy, people say. It is certain that these seven women who were part of the staff of Campus Crusade for Christ International will be deeply missed by family, friends and fellow staff members. But what these women and their families would want you to know is that they are more alive than ever—in heaven. That

These women lost their lives in the Colorado flood...

But they are still alive. They have a message for you.

On July 31 these women hastily left a weekend retreat in the Colorado Rockies. They had been warned to flee a flash flood which was roaring down the canyon. They started out, but never reached the bottom of the canyon alive. More than 100 others also lost their lives in the Big Thompson Canyon that same night.

A tragedy, people say. It is certain that these seven women who were part of the staff of Campus Crusade for Christ International will be deeply missed by family, friends and fellow staff members.

But what these women and their families would want you to know is that they are more alive than ever—in heaven. That they lived a full and wonderful life on this earth. And that they now are better off in the presence of the loving God and Savior whom they served.

If you were to die today, do you know for certain that you would go to heaven? Would you spend eternity in heaven with Christ or separated from Him forever. For those who have a personal relationship with Jesus Christ, death's sting has been taken away. God is our refuge and strength. A very present help in trouble.

He reaches out in love to all men and women, offering His forgiveness, peace and comfort through Jesus Christ. So there is no reason to fear life or death.

Jesus said, "I am the resurrection, and the life; whoever believes in Me shall live even if he dies, and everyone who lives and believes in Me shall never die" (John 11:25,26).

A personal relationship with Jesus Christ doesn't begin at death—but it is available to you now—in life. Twenty-eight other women leaders of Campus Crusade for Christ International left that retreat with these seven. They are still alive—physically as well as spiritually.

But they also have a more keen awareness of the delicate balance between life and death. And more than 5,000 other staff of Campus Crusade for Christ have a keener awareness of life. For them, life is Christ. For the women who died, Christ is life. The message that follows explains what these women want you to know—how you can find new life in Jesus Christ. They had committed themselves to sharing this message in life or in death.

they lived a full and wonderful life on this earth. And that they now are better off in the presence of the loving God and Savior whom they served." Staff members of the movement wanted the world to know that "life is Christ" for them, just as "Christ is life" for their sisters who had died in the flood. A one-track mind? Yes, indeed. As Vonette Bright said of the incident, "As a result of the memorial ad, so many lives were touched that I think each of those seven girls would definitely say, 'Lord, if You can use me in this way, take my life.'"

5 The Berkeley Campus Ministry: A Profile

Saints are persons who make it easier for others to believe in God.

NATHAN SÖDERBLOM

Since the early 1950s, the ministry of Campus Crusade at the University of California, Berkeley has grown and waned at different periods, with new generations of students, during the years leading up to the present. Today, the movement at Cal is strong and has a character all its own. In certain respects, this chapter is hardly typical of the movement in the United States as a whole. But Berkeley isn't a typical American university or city either. The Cal campus is situated within a very liberal and permissive urban environment, with numerous minority ghettos nearby. The San Francisco Bay Area in general probably has one of the most "secular" populations in the country, and the university itself contributes to that "post-Christian" atmosphere. Students at Cal tend to be more liberal in every way than students at most other colleges and universatives too. They are highly individualistic in manners, dress, speech, and attitudes; epitomizing the "do your own thing" philosophy. Students can pretty well do as they please, and live and die without anyone so much as blinking an eye.

On fraternity row, which is booming, pledges and actives have their drunken beer parties just as in the 1950s, while students smoke pot openly in Sproul Plaza or walking down Telgraph Avenue. Casual clothes prevail; this is not a community where coat and tie or a dressy dress are appropriate. Cal students set their own rules. Relatively speaking, they know why they're in college and where they're going. Five nights a week during term, the undergraduate library remains open until 2 A.M., and good seats are hard to find from almost the beginning of each quarter. Everyone seems either to want a job, with a high salary, or plans to go to graduate school. Thus high grades are important again, because good jobs are hard to get and competition for places in graduate school is very stiff indeed.

Students at Cal are skittish, if not outright scared, of movements and organizations as a whole. For decades Berkeley has been a Mecca for new political, social, and religious causes; but today the students here tend to view all of them with skepticism and cynicism, and they usually have an aversion to being identified with any group or movement. Cal students want to be independent, to be their own person, but they are also lonely and want desperately to find a sense of community. With its 30,000 graduate and undergraduate students, Cal is inherently an anonymous institution of higher education, a "factory," albeit a good one. Most Cal students are Californians, and, because California leads the nation in divorces, many of them come from divorced families, which makes it even more difficult for them to find an identity in this sprawling multiversity. Ordinary living situations—dormitories and apartments—offer extremely little in the way of community. Even "dormies" often don't know the students next door, and apartment dwellers also keep mostly to themselves.

The combination of loneliness, competition for grades, and uncertainty about a job and the future make for a great lack of fulfillment within the student population. Many students, therefore, are surprisingly open to anyone who really cares about them personally. For all its excesses, the countercultural Berkeley of the 1960s and early 1970s did have a rather powerful community of people united in their unselfish idealism centered on social justice issues. They wanted to change the world—*together*. But the new conservatism on campus and in the community tends to be self-seeking and self-centered, a product of the fact that the revolution didn't materialize, the world remains the same, and who cares anyhow? The only real issue at Cal today is *me*, and any campus ministry there must now be directed to the individual and his or her anonymity.

John Bruce, a graduate in music of California State University at Long Beach, is director of Campus Crusade at Cal and has served on its staff there since 1970. In one sense, John is typical of the movement's personnel in general—a fraternity man, well-groomed in the context of the casual, hang-loose Berkeley ethos, bright-eyed, aggressive, and self-assured. And he's definitely a pleasant fellow. But like the campus chapter as a whole, John is also very independent and very much his own person, not a carbon copy of anybody. I met him for coffee at the Cal student union complex in May 1978, near the close of the spring quarter and the start of summer vacation. John is about thirty but could pass easily for an older undergraduate or graduate student. And he smiles a lot, too.

The main student union cafeteria just across Sproul Plaza is a favorite gathering place for Campus Crusade students and staff. They are easily recognized there both by their frequent smiles and by the Bibles they often carry with their textbooks. We met two of them in the cafeteria, studying their well-underlined Bibles together between classes, on our way to a quieter group of tables downstairs. They smiled and greeted John as we walked by.

I asked John about his own spiritual pilgrimage and how he became involved with Campus Crusade. "I was raised in the church," he declares. "But when I went away to college I pretty much abandoned any vestige of religion and led a typical hedonistic student life. The Christians on campus told me that if I gave my life to Christ I'd have happiness and joy. Yet that didn't appeal to me, because I felt I already had those things. I was on top of the world, and things were just going fine. During the next few years, however, it became clear to me that the qualities I insisted on in my friends— loyalty, honesty, integrity—were absent from my own life, and it began to bother me. The girl from my home town I'd been dating for four years became a Christian during this time. When I went home to see her, we'd spent a lot of time together, and more time in Bible studies than at the drive-in—which was a real change from the past.

She was involved with Campus Crusade. I met her friends in the local chapter, and there was a real *authenticity* about their lives that impressed me. I came to them as Joe Fraternity, playing all the little games that really impress no one, but there was no authenticity in anything *I* was doing. Nevertheless, they accepted me just as I was, and I really did need that unconditional acceptance. It was these people's concern for me that convinced me, finally, that they were right, and in June 1968 I, too, became a Christian.

"So I joined the Campus Crusade chapter at Long Beach State. I had always planned to be a high school music teacher. But right after graduation I began to see that my goals in life had changed. Comfort, security, and a decent salary were no longer the issues. I was still a relatively young believer, but I could see that the thing that changed my life was knowing Christ in a personal way, and what I enjoyed most was introducing people to that reality. In time, I was struck with the strong conviction that God wanted me to invest my life in other people who would be able to teach still others about Christ. Campus Crusade, of course, seemed the logical place for me to go, and I joined staff in 1970. They placed me at Cal, and I've been here ever since."

But joining staff in Berkeley was only the beginning of John's development in his new calling. "When I first started here as a staff trainee, I was very cocky, and I thought that Campus Crusade was really getting a good deal in me. My trainers were patient with me, however, and after a year of relative failure in my ministry things got better. My campus director just kept on encouraging me and telling me that he really *needed* me here. That was enough, and from the beginning of my second year on staff things began to happen, as I learned how to motivate men and women into a relationship with God and teach them to pour their lives into other people. When I started at Cal, we had about 35 students involved in the ministry—coming to Bible studies, at least. Several years ago we had up to 400 involved in a regular way. Right now there are between 200 and 300. Numbers have changed over the years, but our vision remains the same—finding faithful men and women and investing our lives in them so that they might do the same for others."

Today the Campus Crusade chapter at Cal is one of the largest active student groups of any kind on campus. Each Wednesday evening during term the chapter meets together at Berkeley's First Presbyterian Church for a Bible study led by John Bruce that attracts an average of 100 to 150 students. But that weekly get-together could stand or fall without having a great effect on the ministry as a whole, which centers on one-to-one relationships and small-group activity. "Because most Cal students have an aversion to being identified as a cog in the wheel of a big movement," John says, "the ministry is oriented toward individuals. Our students see their relationship to Campus Crusade as focused on the little group of caring people they meet with. Most of our training takes place in these small 'action groups.' On other campuses, students are more into feeling that they're part of something big—a movement, if you will. So they have what we call a weekly leadership training class, where most of the chapter's content, curriculum, and training are passed down."

I asked John what the eighteen staff members of the Cal chapter do in their ministry. "The staff and student leaders are pretty much doing the same thing," he replied. "Each one is developing his or her own personal ministry. The way they begin doing that, obviously, is by *finding* people to work with. That's where evangelism comes in. Every staff member and student leader selects a specific area of campus life as his or her little mission field. It might be a dorm, a fraternity or sorority, or an athletic team. We focus on winning, building, and sending potential leaders here. Our goal is to reach as many students as we can in each of these areas and raise up disciples to be sent out to win yet others. We use the telephone in setting up personal appointments with students every week. And we also use various kinds of 'religious surveys' to facilitate communication be- tween people who've just met. As a conversation opener, we want to find out what they believe about spiritual things. This helps us know where they're coming from and what they really need. Then we try to get these students into a small, informal group—often in a living area—and begin speaking with them about Christ in a simple, practical, nonthreatening way—meeting them exactly 'where they're at.' Out of the small groups disciples are born whom we build in the faith and send out to win others."

In addition to the regular campus ministry, the Cal chapter of Campus Crusade has under its umbrella a training center for the movement's International Student Ministries. The Berkeley campus has an unusually high concentration of international students (mostly graduates), and ISM seeks to develop a campus ministry of its own geared to the particular needs of internationals. Its director and trainers work under John Bruce's authority, but, in fact, they operate largely as an independent team.

John's own daily schedule is not unlike that of the average American campus ministry director. He gets up usually between 5:30 and 6:00 in the morning, spends a hour and a half to two hours in prayer, followed by about two hours in study, and has appointments with staff and students, generally on campus, that take up another five to six hours each day. John arrives home about 5 P.M. and spends three or four evenings every week teaching the Bible to some group or another—to football players on Tuesdays and to the chapter as a whole on Wednesdays. He also teaches a Bible class at his church on Sunday mornings. In addition to these responsibilities, there are the frequent social activities and retreats that demand his personal involvement. Unlike some parallel campus ministries—among them, Inter-Varsity Christian Fellowship, a student-directed and staff-facilitated movement—Campus Crusade is staff directed and student led, requiring even more staff time. Nevertheless, the students do much of the planning and work, and they decide on and develop their own areas of ministry on the Cal campus.

I asked John about the cultural behavior of students and staff at Berkeley. Do they dance? Drink? "Those really aren't issues for us," he declares, "because we haven't talked about them. Some of us dance, some of us don't. Some of the men and women in fraternities or sororities, for instance, drink on occasion, but again, we don't make an issue of it. As Bill says, 'For the new Christian, we try to put the focus on the positive—on growing in his new relationship with

Christ. We find that the Spirit deals individually with various habits in his life and that many of these habits just fall by the wayside as he grows.' "

The Cal chapter of the movement is even more a "family" than most other chapters. Many of the staff and students actually live together. Several years ago, a benefactor gave an apartment house in Berkeley to Campus Crusade. This is where all the single staff members live, and, until numbers grew too large, it was the place where chapter meetings were held as well. Thirty to forty of the students live together at "the zoo," another apartment house close to campus. But, in general, students are encouraged to live in "the world," in a dormitory or in a fraternity or sorority, for the sake of the ministry's outward reach. "I think that some of the most successful ministries we've had at Cal," John explains, "have been where strong Christians have pledged a sorority or fraternity and have developed close relationships among the gals or guys in that particular house. I can think of one fraternity right now where one of our guys has lived four years. At least *half* of the guys in that house come to his weekly Bible study."

For years, John Bruce had a reputation in Berkeley as a doctrinaire theological conservative, and it stifled his ministry. By and large, he's given that up now. "My own Bible study and personal development had a lot to do with my change of heart in this regard," he says. "I think that we Christians sometimes have to go through a 'Pharisee stage' where we're so into our ministry, so into learning the *truth* about things, that we become very proud of what we've learned. But then we have to move beyond that in order to really accept and love people regardless of our differences. The more I've grown in my faith and in my ministry, the more I've seen that the *test* of a vital relationship with God is not doctrinal rigidity, but love for people. My tendency to allow doctrinal issues to come between me and others often caused them to turn away from the Kingdom—I lacked God's perspective on the situation. The truth should lead us into relationship with people, not *away* from relationship. So I mellowed out. I still have very strong convictions, but—unless it's an absolute *essential*—I really try hard to keep it to myself."

I wanted to know how Bill Bright himself fits into the Berkeley campus ministry. For John, Bill's leadership of the movement is most important, because "he keeps stretching our horizons. He came to us, for example, asking our help with Here's Life just when we were already up to our ears with work. In one sense, we fought him all the way; but as usual, when it was over, we were glad we helped after all. The I found it! campaign probably didn't make a big impact on the secular community in this area, but it certainly did benefit the individuals and churches which were involved. It enabled them to trust God and move out into areas they never would have even thought of apart from their involvement in this particular strategy. And it helped unify many of our local churches in their common witness too. If Bill died tomorrow, it surely wouldn't be a fatal blow for the ministry at Cal, but it *would* slow us down. We really need a shot in the arm from him now and again to keep us on our toes, to enlarge our vision."

THE CHAPTER MEMBERS AND STAFF

We have already discussed at some length the common stereotype of Campus Crusade as a movement of white, upper-middle-class, very straight social and political conservatives who are good looking, perhaps, but not especially bright academically. Despite John Bruce's reputation in Berkeley, I found him far less conservative in lifestyle and cultural attitudes than I expected. Because of the authority structure, staff and students of any given Campus Crusade chapter in the United States tend to share the same outlook on many different issues. To find out exactly where members of the Berkeley chapter stood with respect to politics and culture, and to learn about their backgrounds in general, I administered a brief questionnaire to 108 students and 10 staff attending one of the weekly Wednesday night Bible studies in May 1978. The results of that survey turned out to be most interesting.

Of the staff present that evening, 6 were men, 4 were women. Of the students, 52 were men, 56 were women. Almost all the students were in the 18–23 age bracket, with 16 majoring in the humanities,

30 in the social sciences, 23 in the natural sciences other than engineering, 16 in engineering, and 24 in other areas. Racially, all but one of the staff (an Asian-American) listed themselves as Caucasian. Of the students, 88 were white, 15 Asian-Americans, 2 blacks, 1 Latino, and one "other." Only 29 students listed themselves as fraternity or sorority members, and just 13 were involved in a varsity sport at Cal. In terms of grade point average (4.0 being perfect), 37 of the students had less than a 3.0 (B) average, but 25 had a 3.5 (A minus) average or better (10 listed their G.P.A. as between 3.75-4.0, a truly outstanding record at Cal). Of the sample, 76 students considered themselves at least "fairly active" members of the Campus Crusade chapter (17 were future staff), the others being "casual" in their relationship to the movement, with 13 "visitors" among them. But the attitudes of active members and staff were not much different from those shared by those who were only casually involved with Campus Crusade.

The vast majority of staff (7) and students (81) had become Christians before college. No one denomination was dominant among them, but 19 described themselves as Baptists and 22 as Presbyterians. Of the students, 75 declared that they were active church members. Graduate school was in the plans of 68 of the students—29 hoped to go to law, business, dental, or medical school; 5 to seminary; and 6 contemplated Ph.D. work.

Of the staff, 6 preferred Gerald Ford as president in the 1976 general election; 3 went for Jimmy Carter. Of the students, 42 preferred Ford, 48, Carter. Three members of the staff and 41 students were Republicans; 4 staff and 47 students were Democrats. With respect to basic political philosophy, 2 of the staff and 30 students termed themselves "conservative"; 6 staff and 51 students, "moderate"; 2 staff and 21 students, "liberal"; and 2 students, "radical."

Eighty-six students and 6 staff members came from homes where both parents are still living together. Only 14 students and 2 staff responding indicated that their parents were divorced or separated. Thirty-four students and 7 staff listed neither parent as a college graduate, 20 students and 1 staff member said that one parent had a

B.A. or B.S. degree; 18 students indicated that both parents were college graduates. Two members of the staff and 28 students said that at least one parent had a graduate degree; 8 students said that both their parents had a graduate degree.

Only 2 of the staff and 52 of the students listed both parents as Christians. Of staff and students together, 17 indicated a combined parental annual income of less than $12,000; 23 said between $12,000 and $20,000; 36, between $20,000 and $30,000; 29, between $30,000 and $50,000; and 13, more than $50,000.

In terms of sexual attitudes, chapter staff and students were uniformly conservative. The vast majority felt that premarital intercourse is always wrong. So is homosexual practice. Of the staff, 9 indicated that abortion is wrong unless the mother's life is in danger (one staff person disagreed), and 76 of the students felt the same way. On the proper role of women in church and society, 78 of the students and 7 of the staff agreed that wives must always obey their husbands. None of the staff affirmed that women should ever teach the Bible to men (but 67 of the students disagreed with the staff opinion). One staff member and 27 students were able to approve of the ordination of women if they were intellectually and spiritually qualified.

Finally, I asked the question, "Should Campus Crusade *as a movement* become more active in the fight against 'social sins' such as racism and economic and social injustice?" None of the staff answered affirmatively, but 31 of the students responded "yes."

The Berkeley chapter, then, like the stereotype, *is* predominantly white (with a large minority involvement of Asian-Americans, however), upper-middle-class by income and education of parents, and good looking (yes, indeed). But it is also intelligent and moderate in political outlook. Conservative theology, uniform throughout the movement, doesn't necessarily mean conservative politics as well.

By no means should the aforementioned statistics be taken as representative of the movement in the United States as a whole; after all, Berkeley is an unusual campus and community. Nevertheless, they do offer some concrete evidence that there is probably a great deal more cultural, social, and political diversity within Campus Crusade for Christ than most supporters or detractors imagine.

PART III
THEOLOGY

6 Bill Bright, Pragmatic Theologian of the Holy Spirit

> The Christian church was designed to make aggressive
> movements in every direction—to lift up her voice and put forth
> her energies against iniquity in high and low places—to reform
> individuals, communities, and governments, and never rest until
> the kingdom and the greatness of the kingdom under the whole
> heaven shall be given to the people of the saints of the most High
> God—until every form of iniquity shall be driven from the earth.
>
> CHARLES G. FINNEY, *"Letters on Revivals"*

EVANGELICAL ROOTS: A BRIEF SURVEY

Campus Crusade for Christ as a movement is indeed characterized by a conservative theology and a pragmatic methodology developed by Bill Bright in the course of his ministry. From top to bottom, throughout the organization, this "simple theology," as Bill describes it, and the pragmatic way it is proclaimed and demonstrated give Campus Crusade a distinctive character all its own—a style of theological thinking and action rooted in post-Reformation pietism, revivalism, the nineteenth-century holiness movement, fundamentalism, and postfundamentalist evangelicalism.

After the Civil War, American Protestantism underwent significant changes in its theological character. Darwinian evolution and the new geological theories arguing for a much older earth than earlier notions had allowed challenged the biblical account of creation in seven days. "Higher criticism" of the Bible, stemming from the German universities, questioned the traditional authorship and date of writing of the various books of Scripture as well as their historical reliability in general and the miraculous or supernatural elements they contain in particular. The late nineteenth century also saw the birth of the Social Gospel, a movement led mainly by liberal theologians, pastors, and lay people who sought to bring the ethical teachings of the Old Testament prophets and Jesus himself to bear on the fresh social problems that resulted from rapid urbanization, technological advance, and industrialization. Social Gospel proponents were deeply concerned about increasing urban blight and poverty and about the city dwellers who, with their children, were overworked, underpaid, and housed in intolerable conditions. Seeking to change these circumstances, Social Gospel adherents were not content to wait for changed individuals to create a changed society— an assumption inherent in pietism. They focused their attention, rather, on the "immoral" social and political structures that lay behind the plight of poor city dwellers and argued for a planned structural reform of society as a whole. Some of them envisioned that reform in a moderate welfare-type capitalism; others insisted that socialism was the only possible Christian solution to social and economic injustice, as capitalism was based on the profit motive that exalts self-gain and selfishness, characteristics they felt were incompatible with the life and teachings of Jesus.

The intelligensia of American Protestantism—seminary professors and denominational officials—gradually made their peace with higher biblical criticism and the new scientific theories. Liberalism as a theological movement in the United States developed during the late nineteenth century and finally captured most of the Protestant seminaries and denominational hierarchies in the twentieth century. The liberals very quickly adjusted to the worldly culture by endeavoring to hold beliefs in harmony with science (seeing God behind the evolutionary process, for instance) while attempting to retain the core of religious belief. They emphasized the immanence of God in the world (God with us, "right here, right now") rather than his transcendance (God's "otherness, being out there"). And in the context of nineteenth-century optimism, before the two world wars, they believed in the possibility of the progressive moral improve-

This 1940s "Clark Gable" photo of Bill sat on Vonette's dresser during their dating years.

Bill and Vonette after their wedding in 1947.

Bill introduces his new bride to the college and young career department at Hollywood Presbyterian Church, of which he was president.

The president and founder of Bright's Fancy Foods sits proudly with some of his product in 1947.

Miss Henrietta Mears, Director of Christian Education, Hollywood Presbyterian Church.

Through large group evangelistic meetings, Bill found new people who were interested in learning more about Christianity and a personal relationship with Christ. These meetings also played a key part in building the enthusiasm of students and staff who were trying to reach their campuses for Christ.

Bill believed that the small group meeting was ideal for discipling others. Here he leads a cell meeting in a house at UCLA in the early 1950's. Small groups are still the essence of Campus Crusade's ministry today.

Bill's early ministry involved several all-American football players from UCLA. On the left is Don Moomaw, three times All-American and presently senior pastor of Bel Air Presbyterian Church, California. On the right is Bob Davenport, two times All-American, now founder and president of Wondering Wheels, an international Christian ministry to youth.

Bill and Vonette, in the lower left of photo, host the 1955 staff training of Campus Crusade at Douglas Hall, UCLA.

From the very beginning Bill recognized the power of the media. Here he shows Rafer Johnson, former Olympic decathlon champion, one of the early issues of a Campus Crusade newspaper which proclaims his plans to help reach the world for Christ.

Arrowhead Springs, the international headquarters of Campus Crusade, is located in the San Bernardino mountains.

Bill and his staff: first row, from left to right: Glenn Plate, Don Myers, Bailey Marks, Kundan Massey, Bill Bright, Vonette Bright, Sergio Garcia, Bud Hinkson, Kalevi Lehtinin, Marvin Kehler. Second row, from left to right: Frank Obien, Steve Douglass, Larry Poland, Paul Eshleman, Swede Anderson. Missing from photo: Kent Hutcheson, Ted Martin.

Directors of Affairs:
Kundan Massey—
Middle East

Don Myers—Africa

Kalevi Lehtinen—Europe

Bailey Marks—Asia

Sergio Garcia—
Latin America

Marvin Kehler—Canada

In 1966 when Timothy Leary started his philosophy for the drug culture, Campus Crusade for Christ staff were right next to the platform giving the students another alternative.

A photo of the *Right On* (Christian magazine) staff (now *Rãdix*), an arm of the Christian World Liberation Front. Seated from left to right: Steve Sparks, David Gill, Sharon Gallagher, Jack Buckley. Standing from left to right: Paul Lee, Keith Criss, Jess Grijaiba, Karen Hoyt, Jack Sparks, Elizabeth Chaffee, Jerry Exel, Howard Criss. Seated on roof: Bryan Richter, Arnie Bernstein.

AIA basketball star Wayne Smith sinks a basket against some NBA all-stars.

Over one million people attended the outdoor meetings of Explo '74 in South Korea.

Bill is applauded after speaking to the state legislature of Texas in 1975. With Bill are, left, Governor Dolph Briscoe, Bright, Dr. Charles Malik, Professor of Philosophy, American University of Beirut, Lebanon and former president of the General Assembly of the United Nations.

Bill prays with members of the Soviet Baptist Union at the site of a cemetery for war heroes.

Bill speaks by interpreter at the First Baptist Church of Moscow at one of fifteen speaking engagements during a 1977 trip to the Soviet Union.

The Big Thompson flood in Colorado claimed the lives of seven staff women.

Diane Farmer, Agape staff member in Liberia, Africa, teaches her class basic English. She is one of 139 Agape staff serving in vocational, technical and medical teams around the world.

Bill announces the Here's Life Funding Campaign at a Washington, D.C. press conference. Seated at the table, left to right: Wallace Johnson, Bill Bright, Nelson Bunker Hunt, Dale Evans Rogers, Roy Rogers.

Bill shares the Here's Life strategy with pastors and Christian leaders of Jakarta at the city-wide vision meeting held on October 20, 1977, at the Indonesia Sheraton, Jakarta.

An "I found it!" worker shares Christ with a gas station attendant.

An "I found it!" telephone center.

Today

ment of human society. The liberals studied the Bible critically and scientifically, viewing it as the historical record of the development of Jewish and early Christian religion, not as the infallible word of God. Placing heavy emphasis on reason, they did not believe in the supernaturally miraculous and were convinced that all elements of life were controlled by natural processes. As a whole, liberals championed the Social Gospel.

Fundamentalism, a movement within American Protestantism that peaked in the mid-1920s, was the major force responding to liberalism. Its roots are to be found, first of all, in pietism. By the early seventeenth century, the mainstream of post-Reformation Lutheranism had already become channeled in rigid doctrinal and sacramental forms, and Calvinism had settled into dogmatic legalism. The early pietists in Germany sought to restore to the life of the Reformation churches the original emphasis of the Reformation on heartfelt personal religion against the rationalistic doctrinal orthodoxy that had become dominant in those same churches. Pietism began with the organization of "conventicles"—small groups of people who gathered regularly for Bible study. These groups were the vehicle by which the movement spread throughout Protestant Europe and the United States, emphasizing individual regeneration (new birth), emotional warmth rather than correct doctrine per se, personal godliness and denial of "the world" (piety), and the universal spiritual priesthood of believers. Pietism engendered philanthropic institutions of various sorts, the establishment of Protestant foreign mission work, and the composition of some of the best loved hymns of the church. It also fostered the conviction that only regenerated individuals can build a truly righteous society.

Revivalism was a second major force that influenced fundamentalism. Originally conceived as a method of reviving the spiritual life of believers and churches (its emphasis on evangelism, winning the lost, came later), the movement started in the Middle Colonies early in the eighteenth century and quickly spread to New England under the leadership of Jonathan Edwards in Northampton, Massachusetts. George Whitefield, who made several trips from England to the United States between 1738 and 1770, was one of the principal unifiers in this First Great Awakening which was felt throughout the Colonies. Revivalism flourished with great preachers like Charles G. Finney and Dwight L. Moody in the nineteenth century and Billy Sunday and Billy Graham in the twentieth century. Like pietism more generally, revivalism centered its focus on renewal of the personal life of faith, on "warming the heart" of individual believers, and, in its later development, on reaching nonbelievers.

In the course of the nineteenth century, American revivalism itself was affected, on the one hand, by dispensationalism, a school of theology originating in the early 1800s in Great Britain with J.N. Darby. It saw human society getting progressively worse until the Second Coming, which was "imminent." Efforts to create a more righteous social order were hopeless. Only God, by his decisive action at the end of history, could alleviate the situation by establishing his millennial reign on earth. God would consummate his Kingdom in his own good time, which was fast approaching. Dispensationalists, furthermore, were premillennialists, believing that Christ would return *before* the thousand years of peace and righteousness on earth. But many of the revivalists in the nineteenth century, Finney among them, were postmillennialists, convinced that Christ would return *after* the millennium, giving believers an opportunity to help build the Kingdom in anticipation of its final consummation. The relative peace and prosperity of the nineteenth century produced an optimism that fostered both postmillennialism and the Social Gospel.

Another influence on revivalism in the nineteenth century was the holiness movement, itself rooted deeply in pietism. Holiness theology derives largely from John Wesley and early Methodism. For the most part, it stressed Christian perfection, or personal holiness, as a second blessing—or second work of grace—after conversion, an instantaneous experience in which a believer is totally cleansed and freed from all sin. By and large, the holiness movement rested on Arminian theology, which, in contrast to Calvinism, emphasized free will rather than predestination and human perfectibility in Christ rather than total depravity. But the movement also had a moderate Calvinistic branch in England, spearheaded by the annual Keswick conferences held to promote spiritual renewal and practical holiness—a *process* of life after the crisis of conversion rather than an instantaneous second work of grace. Dwight L. Moody, in the course of his visits to England in the late nineteenth century, influenced the Keswick movement deeply.

Fundamentalism embraced pietism's stress on the religion of the heart and separation from the world, revivalism's technique of mass evangelism to revive the spiritual life, the holiness movement's concern for holy living, and dispensational theology's focus on the imminent Second Coming of Christ. It advanced throughout the late nineteenth and early twentieth centuries in opposition to the growing "threat" of liberalism. The more fundamentalism advanced, however, the more it reacted against liberalism and everything it stood for. Increasingly, it condemned the Social Gospel in its entirety because it was led by theological liberals and seemed to neglect the urgency of personal regeneration, the only effective means of restructuring sinful society by regenerating sinful men and women. Furthermore, fundamentalist revivals and prophetic Bible conferences became determined to defend the faith and, in so doing, lapsed into a rigid doctrinal dogmatism that was other-worldly, rejected even the good elements of human culture, and took on a decidedly antiintellectual and separatist spirit in its ecclesiastical relationships.*

*The name *fundamentalist,* coined in 1920, derives from a series of twelve booklets by prominent conservative theologians, setting forth the fundamental doctrines of Christian orthodoxy, and distributed to some 3 million Christian leaders throughout the world over a five-year period from 1910 to 1915. These doctrines were finally summarized in five articles of faith adopted by the General Assembly of the Presbyterian Church in the U.S.A.—now The United Presbyterian Church in the U.S.A.—in 1910 and reaffirmed in 1916 and 1923. The doctrines focused on the "supernatural" aspects of the Christian faith denied by liberals—the inerrancy of Scripture in the original documents, the deity and virgin birth of Jesus, his substitutionary atonement for sin, his physical resurrection, and his miracle-working power. In addition, fundamentalism was also characterized by a belief in the natural depravity of men and women (revealing its strong Calvinistic bias), justification by faith alone (in contrast to Roman Catholicism and works-oriented Arminian Protestantism), the personal (bodily) return of Christ, and a literal heaven and hell.

By the early 1940s, fundamentalism as a movement—in its opposi-
tionist posture—had become so intransigent, so narrow in its theological, cultural, and political attitudes, that a group of young
intellectuals within the movement's ranks raised a strong voice of
protest. There had always been responsible "conservatives" among
the fundamentalists who sought to preserve a generally open spirit
and warm disposition even in the face of continuing doctrinal battles.
But their irenic, conciliatory stance ceased to be recognized by the
movement's leaders. Thus the young fundamentalist intellectuals
(Carl F. H. Henry and Harold Ockenga among them), aided by
sympathetic church leaders, began to promulgate a "new evangelicalism," which would retain belief in the fundamentals of the faith
and preserve the best elements of both pietism and revivalism but
would reject the extremes of separatism, antiintellectualism, and
social unconcern (reflected in political ultraconservatism) characteristic of fundamentalism. In other words, the new evangelicals
favored the kind of evangelical Christianity epitomized by the
Wesleyan revival in eighteenth-century England and by the eigh-
teenth- and nineteenth-century revivals in the United States that
focused on simple regeneration through faith in Christ alone and on
the serious and strenuous imitation of the life of Jesus Christ. In 1942,
these new evangelical theologians and church leaders founded the
National Association of Evangelicals as an evangelical counterpart to
the liberal Federal Council of Churches (now National Council of
Churches). In 1947, they established Fuller Seminary, and in 1949,
the Evangelical Theological Society. Also in 1949, they began to
gravitate toward Billy Graham and his ecumenical evangelism that
repudiated evangelistic meetings of a separatist nature, those in
which nonfundamentalists were not allowed to participate in leadership. Finally, in 1956, the new evangelicals founded *Christianity
Today,* a biweekly magazine that became the "official" mouthpiece
of modern evangelical Christianity.

INFLUENCES ON BILL BRIGHT'S THOUGHT

Hollywood Pres., from its beginnings, was marked by a conciliatory and open theological conservatism. Its ministers, schooled in the

best traditions of revivalism and Protestant orthodoxy, did not try to get the church to leave its parent, and increasingly inclusive, denomination (now The United Presbyterian Church in the U.S.A.), even though they were fully aware of liberal gains within its ranks. And its upper-middle-class congregation of educated professional people did not wish to be known as world-rejecting separatists or sectarians. Thus Hollywood Pres. greeted the new evangelicalism with enthusiasm. Bill Bright's theology, and that of the movement he founded, is very much a product not only of his seminary education but also of his deep involvement in Hollywood Pres. and its struggle to keep the orthodox faith alive in the context of the warm heart and loving spirit inherent in evangelical Christianity.

Bill's theology was influenced, first of all, by his background on the ranch in Coweta, Oklahoma. The Protestant work ethic, whereby God blesses an individual who works hard in a righteous manner, was operative in his life from the very beginning. Hard work made him one of the most outstanding young men in Coweta and later in college, and it helped him produce a successful business in a few short years. Mary Lee Rohl Bright, Bill's mother, was a true Wesleyan, nurtured in the Methodist Church and in its holiness tradition. She demonstrated to Bill that holiness is a real possibility for a Spirit-filled Christian, and he never forgot it.

Bill Bright brought with him to Hollywood Pres. a pragmatic spirit, nurtured by his own successful business career. As a philosophy—a very American philosophy—pragmatism has been articulated best by the eminent philosopher William James. For him, and for Bill too, pragmatism means that ideas are true insofar as they are satisfactory; to be satisfactory, ideas must be consistent with other ideas, conformable to facts, and subject to the practical tests of experience. If it works, it is true. In Bill's thinking, theology must be tested by experience. If it works in an individual, if it changes his or her life, it is true. Theology "proves itself" by being functional not by fostering mere metaphysical speculation. Hence in his own study, Bill Bright has been more influenced by practical devotional writings than by systematic theology, and he has been more impressed by the lives of the great evangelists (like Finney and Moody) than by what they preached.

At Hollywood Pres., of course, Henrietta Mears deeply influenced Bill's theology. She had been raised in W.B. Riley's First Baptist Church of Minneapolis. Riley was a dedicated Calvinistic Baptist and an active fundamentalist (the primary force behind the World's Christian Fundamentals Association, founded in 1919). He was also, on the whole, a separatist. Near the end of his life, in fact, Riley officially broke with the Northern Baptist Convention (now American Baptist Churches in the U.S.A.) over the inclusion of liberals in its denominational leadership. In coming to Hollywood, Mears rejected Riley's dogmatism and separatism but not his emphasis on evangelism. Teacher felt strongly that evangelism is the heart of the gospel and salvation is the ultimate issue in life. She, too, was a pragmatist. Her science background proved to her that answers can be found to even the most complex questions, and truth is borne out by practical experience. Her own success in increasing Sunday school attendance dramatically in a short time was proof. What she taught was true, and that truth was demonstrated to her clearly by the large number of students her teaching influenced to the point where their lives were completely changed.

Partly because of her upper-class status and background and partly because of her spirit, Mears always de-emphasized peripheral, nonessential doctrines as a test of faith. She was never a sectarian. Although a Calvinist, Teacher did not waste time speculating about the elect and the damned, predestination and irresistible grace. Rather, it was one's life and how it was lived that counted for God not one's pristine orthodoxy. The early Sunday school curricula developed by Gospel Light Publications tended to be moderately dispensational in outlook, but Mears did not push dispensationalism on her students. She always had a high regard for education, and prided herself on the number of her students who went to the best colleges and universities, and to Princeton Seminary, despite the school's increasing liberal character through the years of her ministry. Henrietta Mears liked having a good time. She traveled widely, enjoyed parties and formal banquets, and lived in Bel Air; but she was also a pietist in the best sense of the word. Personal devotion—regular prayer and Bible study—was an integral part of her daily life. Pietism was also an integral feature of the Hollywood Pres. college department, reflected not only in the devotional life of its members but in their personal behavior as well. In those days, activities such as drinking, smoking, and dancing were considered worldly. A Christian party was characterized—even in Bel Air—by the absence of such worldly behavior, because believing Christians had to be distinguished from the world. Nevertheless, Teacher was never a moralist or a legalist. She didn't condemn those whose behavior was different from her own. Henrietta Mears just lived her life for others, and Bill Bright and the other Mears boys followed that example.

While in seminary at Princeton and Fuller, Bill spent a great deal of time in practical Christian ministry, as chairman of the Hollywood Pres. deputation teams, for instance. And he was probably formed more by that experience of evangelism than by the formal classroom training he received. Bill did not complain about the critical tools employed in both seminaries to understand the Bible, because his professors were people of great faith whose words and lives inspired and encouraged him in his own spiritual development. And the fact that Princeton's president at the time, John MacKay, was being accused by right-wing forces of having more "communist front" affiliations than any religious leader of his generation did not stop Bill from praying with him on numerous occasions.

Bill Bright, like Charles Colson more recently, has been deeply influenced by C.S. Lewis' classic apologetic work, *Mere Christianity,* which was originally a series of radio lectures for the BBC. Lewis was certainly not a pietist. He thoroughly enjoyed life at high table at Magdalen College, Oxford, and his regular meetings with the Oxford literary establishment at the local pub. Indeed, Lewis was a literary critic of high esteem as well as an extremely competent lay theologian. His apologetics not only argued for the truth of basic Christian orthodoxy, they also pointed to a higher level of life for the believer who "wants everything." In *Mere Christianity* he declares:

> Give up yourself, and you will find your real self. Lose your life and
> you will save it. Submit to death, death of your ambitions and favourite
> wishes every day and death of your body in the end: submit with every

fibre of your being, and you will find eternal life. Keep back nothing. Nothing that you have not given away will ever really be yours. . . . Look for yourself, and you will find in the long run only hatred, loneliness, rage, ruin, and decay. But look for Christ and you will find him, and with him everything else thrown in.

Bright also has a special attraction to the writings of James S. Stewart, professor emeritus of New Testament language and theology at the University of Edinburgh and a former moderator of the Church of Scotland. Stewart was a preacher of renown—an evangelical liberal in the tradition of William Barclay, the famous Bible expositor and commentator, who appeals to conservatives and liberals alike. Stewart, an "enlightened" Scottish Presbyterian Calvinist, wrote many devotional works, believed strongly in evangelism, and was a force for conciliation and unity in a climate of theological battles both in his own country and abroad.

Finally, Bill was influenced deeply by Andrew Murray, the nineteenth-century Dutch Reformed minister and South African ecclesiastical statesman par excellence, who was, in turn, influenced by the British Keswick conferences and the Spirit-led theology they espoused. Keswick, unlike true Wesleyan holiness theology, did not stand for the complete eradication of sin in the life of a Spirit-filled believer. Rather, the movement believed in sin's suppression by the faithful believer to the point that he or she could have victory over the ever-present reality of sin in the life of Christians—a Calvinist rather than an Arminian notion of the nature of holiness. When a person is filled with the Spirit of God, he or she immediately receives "power for service" (Acts 1:8) not sinlessness (though Keswick people did aim at perfection).

Murray was a pietist both in lifestyle and in devotion. Indeed, he strongly favored Bible study, prayer, and fellowship in small groups of people—the pietistic conventicle model—wherein the Holy Spirit builds up faith and enlarges vision much more than the Spirit does in the solitary devotion of a single believer. Murray explains:

> It is a well-known fact that in proportion as the unity of the body is exhibited and fostered in love and fellowship, the unity of the Spirit is also experienced more powerfully. When the Spirit of God is found working

with power, visions are instantaneously obtained which otherwise would only have come after the lapse of years, and we are strengthened to acts of faith and consecration for which we have longed, and longed in vain, for many months past. That is because the Lord has said, "Where two or three are gathered together in My name, there I am in the midst of them." Solitude, however indispensable, is not sufficient.

As we mentioned earlier, Bill Bright has been influenced by these men and women of faith more because of their lives and the lives they influenced than because of their scholarly erudition. Furthermore, he has been deeply impressed by the fact that these Christians all insisted that true commitment to Christ demands absolute obedience to his commands and absolute selflessness. If Jesus was "the man for others," in Dietrich Bonhoeffer's words, then we, too, ought to follow his example.

BEYOND DOGMATISM

Dogmatism may be defined as a fixed, arrogant, or arbitrary belief, accompanied by unwillingness to examine its grounds or to modify it for any reason. In conservative Protestantism, dogmatism has focused on a rigid form of orthodoxy, right doctrine, and the systematic exposition of that doctrine, requiring an intellectual assent to it. For many fundamentalists, assent to the five fundamentals, interpreted in *the fundamentalist way,* has been absolutely essential for salvation and has functioned as a test of faith as well. *Legalism* is to conduct what dogmatism is to doctrine or belief. It signifies conformity to a prescribed code of rules of conduct missing the inner spirit or purpose of the rules and degenerating into a barren observance of externals. Legalism stands opposed both to pragmatism and to salvation by grace because it requires obedience to rules without regard to consequences (does it work?) and, indirectly at least, rests the claim to salvation on good works (i.e., obeying the rules).

Bill Bright has never been either a dogmatist or a legalist. Apart from the fact that Campus Crusade does have an "orthodox" statement of faith to which all staff members must subscribe (it is not imposed on all Christians), Bill has founded and directed a Christian organization that is remarkably nondoctrinal in character. It is extremely difficult to find systematic doctrinal formulations of any kind in his writings. And this is one reason many theologians term Campus Crusade's theology as simplistic or superficial. Bill was nurtured in one of the most nondogmatic evangelical churches in the country. The issue for Henrietta Mears was salvation, and she was quite willing to let her students work out their own salvation after she had taught them her opinion, based on the message not the letter of Scripture. Like Bill Bright himself, Teacher was very evangelistic. For her, to use Bill's phrasing, the focus of all Christian ministry was winning, building, and sending—not the learning of a prescribed list of immutable doctrines that must be accepted in a prescribed manner at the peril of one's eternal salvation.

Bill Bright believes strongly that the Bible is the Word of God written, but he stresses the need for the Holy Spirit to apply the word to individual lives before there is any "quickening power." Bright explains that "the Holy Spirit makes relevant the Word of God when I need it. It is a *living* Book inspired by the Holy Spirit. And the only person who can understand the Bible is one who is controlled by the Holy Spirit." Bill is more than willing to allow the Spirit to work in an individual's mind and heart any way the Spirit chooses. Indeed, he feels that the church—Presbyterian, Baptist, Methodist, Episcopal, or whatever—not Campus Crusade, bears the responsibility for training new converts in the fine points of doctrine. A committed high church Episcopalian can be just as faithful a disciple as a conservative Baptist. Right action in the discipleship process bears testimony to the truth of one's doctrine—a very ecumenical stance to say the least.

Bill is even less of a legalist than a dogmatist. There are few standing policies or immutable rules of any kind in his movement. This has been true from the beginning, which is one reason antinomianism became a problem within Campus Crusade in the late 1960s. For instance, Bright has encouraged his U.S. staff members not to drink alcoholic beverages at all, but he has consistently refused to set a written policy against that activity for the movement in general. In Europe, for example, where drinking wine or beer is more customary than drinking water, even among the most dedicated Christians, Bill puts no pressure on his national staff to refrain from drinking, though he admonishes them not to flaunt their freedom in a way that would make other staff or Christians "stumble." Again, the ultimate issue is salvation, and the method is people, not rules—being all things to all men and women so that I might win a few. There is much more freedom of lifestyle in Campus Crusade than most outsiders are aware of. In terms of dress, recreation, eating and drinking habits, and the like, staff members do try to live in conformity with the best in the given culture of their ministry as recommended by their superiors. But culture differs dramatically around the world and even in the United States. To discern the freedom of lifestyle within the movement, one need only visit staff members in Germany or Scandinavia or those who work in the black community in this country. One prominent black staff worker in America puts it this way: "I'm still free to be me. I appreciate the fact that when I joined staff, nobody tried to squeeze me into a mold. It's very much a team effort, but Campus Crusade appreciates creativity and does everything possible to encourage you to develop your personal potential."

AGGRESSIVE EVANGELISM

Although Bill and Campus Crusade are not dogmatic in doctrine or legalistic in lifestyle, and although the movement's theology insists that God's method is people, the organization does utilize a well-conceived and highly structured methodology to get the gospel out. One important element in that methodology, and a hallmark of the movement as a whole, is aggressive evangelism. In Bill's words, "Aggressive evangelism is simply *taking the initiative* to share Christ in the power of the Holy Spirit and leave the results to God. We make a special point that aggressive evangelism does not mean *being* offensive; it does mean *taking* the offensive. Everywhere we go we tell everyone who will listen about Christ. And I assume when I'm alone with a person, even for just a few minutes, I am there by divine appointment. I have the privilege, not out of a sense of legalism, but out of a sense of gratitude and love for Christ, as a matter of obedience, to share the good news. In fact, my role is not to make converts at all—that's the Holy Spirit's responsibility. The Spirit uses committed followers of Christ as a vehicle to proclaim and demonstrate the gospel. If people don't want to listen, I don't press. We teach those whom we train never to argue, never to badger, never to press for a decision. We want to talk with those who will listen, trusting the Holy Spirit to change their lives."

As part of the movement's methodology, aggressive evangelism can be distinguished from friendship evangelism, used on campus,

A typical perception of Crusade's aggressive evangelism reflected by Crusade staff cartoonist Steve Becker.

for example, by Inter-Varsity Christian Fellowship. Friendship evangelism means that a believer builds a relationship over a period of time, and after he or she has won the right to be heard, the opportunity to share the gospel in conversation is a natural result. In particular situations that warrant it, Campus Crusade does employ friendship evangelism, at least to a degree. With international students in the United States, for instance, many communication barriers must be overcome before the gospel can be adequately proclaimed. In this case, demonstration of the gospel precedes proclamation. With aggressive evangelism, the sequence is reversed.

Fundamental to the theology and methodology of Bill Bright and Campus Crusade for Christ is a little booklet entitled *Have You Heard of the Four Spiritual Laws?* about 250 million copies of which have been distributed throughout the world in every major language since 1965. In the middle 1950s, Bill decided that the movement needed a standardized evangelistic tool that staff could use in their witnessing, a device by which the basics of the gospel could be presented to those who were willing to listen. He began by writing a twenty-minute presentation for staff to memorize, "God's Plan for Your Life," focusing on the claims of Jesus Christ—who he is, why he came, how men and women can know him. "God's Plan" was Campus Crusade's first written how-to-do-it material, a simple, practical exposition of how to become a Christian. As far as Bill was concerned, this how-to-do-it approach worked, and it became the model for almost all subsequent evangelistic and training materials published by the movement. It was pragmatic.

The presentation of "God's Plan" itself seemed effective to Bill, but he also discovered that a shorter, even more basic, evangelistic tool was needed. Thus he prepared a condensed outline of "God's Plan," complete with Scripture verses and diagrams, and asked his staff to memorize it. But as the movement and its staff grew in numbers, a decision was made in 1965 to print a booklet for easy staff use and wider distribution. The name *Four Spiritual Laws* was used, because the device was originally aimed at college and university students who, as a result of their training in science (emphasized more in the early 1960s, perhaps, than now) already were aware of

Just as there are physical laws that govern the physical universe, so are there spiritual laws which govern your relationship with God.

LAW ONE

GOD **LOVES** YOU, AND OFFERS A WONDERFUL **PLAN** FOR YOUR LIFE.

(References should be read in context from the Bible wherever possible.)

God's Love

"For God so loved the world, that He gave His only begotten Son, that whoever believes in Him should not perish, but have eternal life" (John 3:16).

God's Plan

(Christ speaking) "I came that they might have life, and might have it abundantly" (that it might be full and meaningful) (John 10:10).

Why is it that most people are not experiencing the abundant life?

Because. . .

LAW TWO

MAN IS **SINFUL** AND **SEPARATED** FROM GOD. THEREFORE, HE CANNOT KNOW AND EXPERIENCE GOD'S LOVE AND PLAN FOR HIS LIFE.

Man Is Sinful

"For all have sinned and fall short of the glory of God" (Romans 3:23).

Man was created to have fellowship with God; but, because of his stubborn self-will, he chose to go his own independent way and fellowship with God was broken. This self-will, characterized by an attitude of active rebellion or passive indifference, is evidence of what the Bible calls sin.

Man Is Separated

"For the wages of sin is death" (spiritual separation from God) (Romans 6:23).

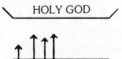

This diagram illustrates that God is holy and man is sinful. A great gulf separates the two. The arrows illustrate that man is continually trying to reach God and the abundant life through his own efforts, such as a good life, philosophy or religion.

The third law explains the only way to bridge this gulf. . .

LAW THREE

JESUS CHRIST IS GOD'S **ONLY** PROVISION FOR MAN'S SIN. THROUGH HIM YOU CAN KNOW AND EXPERIENCE GOD'S LOVE AND PLAN FOR YOUR LIFE.

He Died in Our Place

"But God demonstrates His own love toward us, in that while we were yet sinners, Christ died for us" (Romans 5:8).

He Rose from the Dead

"Christ died for our sins. . .He was buried. . .He was raised on the third day, according to the Scriptures. . .He appeared to Peter, then to the twelve. After that He appeared to more than five hundred. . ." (I Corinthians 15:3-6).

He Is the Only Way to God

"Jesus said to him, 'I am the way, and the truth, and the life; no one comes to the Father, but through Me'" (John 14:6).

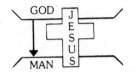

This diagram illustrates that God has bridged the gulf which separates us from God by sending His Son, Jesus Christ, to die on the cross in our place to pay the penalty for our sins.

It is not enough just to know these three laws. . .

LAW FOUR

WE MUST INDIVIDUALLY **RECEIVE** JESUS CHRIST AS SAVIOR AND LORD; THEN WE CAN KNOW AND EXPERIENCE GOD'S LOVE AND PLAN FOR OUR LIVES.

We Must Receive Christ

"But as many as received Him, to them He gave the right to become children of God, even to those who believe in His name" (John 1:12).

We Receive Christ through Faith

"For by grace you have been saved through faith; and that not of yourselves, it is the gift of God; not as a result of works, that no one should boast" (Ephesians 2:8,9).

When We Receive Christ, We Experience a New Birth.

(Read John 3:1-8.)

We Receive Christ by Personal Invitation

(Christ is speaking): "Behold, I stand at the door and knock; if any one hears My voice and opens the door, I will come in to him" (Revelation 3:20).

Receiving Christ involves turning from self to God (repentance and trusting Christ to come into our lives to forgive our sins and to make us the kind of person He wants us to be. Just to agree intellectually that Jesus Christ is the Son of God and that He died on the cross for our sins is not enough. Nor is it enough to have an emotional experience. We receive Jesus Christ by faith, as an act of the will.

These two circles represent two kinds of lives:

SELF-DIRECTED LIFE

S—Self on the throne

†—Christ is outside the life

•Interests are directed
    by self, often resulting in
    discord and frustration

CHRIST-DIRECTED LIFE

†—Christ is in the life
  and on the throne
S—Self is yielding to Christ
●—Interests are directed
  by Christ, resulting in
  harmony with God's plan.

Which circle best represents your life?

Which circle would you like to have represent your life?

The following explains how you can receive Christ:

YOU CAN RECEIVE CHRIST RIGHT NOW BY FAITH THROUGH PRAYER

(Prayer is talking with God)

God knows your heart and is not so concerned with your words as He is with the attitude of your heart. The following is a suggested prayer:

"Lord Jesus, I need You. Thank You for dying on the cross for my sins. I open the door of my life and receive You as my Savior and Lord. Thank You for forgiving my sins and giving me eternal life. Take control of the throne of my life. Make me the kind of person You want me to be."

Does this prayer express the desire of your heart?

If it does, pray this prayer right now, and Christ will come into your life, as He promised.

the physical laws that govern the universe. Bill felt that they also needed to know about the spiritual laws that govern men's and women's relationship with God. These include: (1) God loves you, and offers a wonderful plan for your life. (2) Man is sinful and separated from God. Therefore, he cannot know and experience God's love and plan for his life. (3) Jesus Christ is God's *only* provision for man's sin—through him you can know and experience God's love and plan for your life; and (4) We must individually *receive* Jesus Christ as Savior and Lord; then we can know and experience God's love and plan for our lives. Simple, yes. And notice that a free choice—an act of the will—is required of a person to appropriate God's love and plan. That plan simply is not effective in an individual's life until he or she chooses to experience it.

At the start, before the printed booklet came off the press, there were only three spiritual laws, beginning with the negative concept that men and women are sinful and separated from God—the typical fundamentalist starting point. But Bill was not satisfied with the first law as it stood. "Why not start where God starts, with his love?" he thought. "I had been drawn to Christ originally because I was overwhelmed with God's love. The love of God had been the basis of my presentation of the Gospel ever since I had become a Christian. I wanted everyone to know how much God loves him and that God has a wonderful plan for the life of everyone who will accept his plan." At the time, this idea was seen as highly controversial by many conservative Christians. They felt that, by not beginning with human sinfulness, Bill had diluted the gospel. Perhaps he had even "gone liberal." Nevertheless, the founder of Campus Crusade never regretted the new first law. In fact, it sums up in one sentence the thrust of his whole theology and sense of mission in the world.

The *Four Spiritual Laws* is probably one of the most utilized and imitated tracts in the world today. Even the United Church of Christ, one of America's most liberal denominations, has incorporated the basic concepts involved here in its new evangelism training manual—an ingenious cross-cultural adaptation in the language and cultural context of United Church people.

Prior to the *Four Spiritual Laws* booklet, two evangelistic letters

EVERY DAY CAN BE AN EXCITING ADVENTURE FOR THE CHRISTIAN who knows the reality of being filled with the Holy Spirit and who lives constantly, moment by moment, under His gracious direction.

The Bible tells us that there are three kinds of people.

1. NATURAL MAN
(One who has not received Christ)

"But a natural man does not accept the things of the Spirit of God; for they are foolishness to him, and he cannot understand them, because they are spiritually appraised" (I Corinthians 2:14).

SELF-DIRECTED LIFE
S—Ego or finite self is on the throne
†—Christ is outside the life
•—Interests are directed by self, often resulting in discord and frustration

2. SPIRITUAL MAN
(One who is directed and empowered by the Holy Spirit)

"But he who is spiritual appraises all things . . ." (I Corinthians 2:15).

CHRIST-DIRECTED LIFE
†—Christ is in the life and on the throne
S—Self is yielding to Christ
•—Interests are directed by Christ, resulting in harmony with God's plan

2

3. CARNAL MAN
(One who has received Christ, but who lives in defeat because he trusts in his own efforts to live the Christian life)

SELF-DIRECTED LIFE
S—Self is on the throne
†—Christ dethroned and not allowed to direct the life
•—Interests are directed by self, often resulting in discord and frustration

"And I, brethren, could not speak to you as to spiritual men, but as to carnal men, as to babes in Christ. I gave you milk to drink, not solid food; for you were not yet able to receive it. Indeed, even now you are not yet able, for you are still carnal. For since there is jealousy and strife among you, are you not fleshly, and are you not walking like mere men?" (I Corinthians 3:1-3).

3

1. GOD HAS PROVIDED FOR US AN ABUNDANT AND FRUITFUL CHRISTIAN LIFE.

Jesus said, "I came that they might have life, and might have it abundantly" (John 10:10).

"I am the vine, you are the branches; he who abides in Me, and I in him, he bears much fruit; for apart from Me you can do nothing" (John 15:5).

"But the fruit of the Spirit is love, joy, peace, patience, kindness, goodness, faithfulness, gentleness, self-control; against such things there is no law" (Galatians 5:22, 23).

"But you shall receive power when the Holy Spirit has come upon you; and you shall be My witnesses both in Jerusalem, and in all Judea and Samaria, and even to the remotest part of the earth" (Acts 1:8).

4

THE SPIRITUAL MAN—Some personal traits which result from trusting God:

Christ-centered
Empowered by the Holy Spirit
Introduces others to Christ
Effective prayer life
Understands God's Word
Trusts God
Obeys God

Love
Joy
Peace
Patience
Kindness
Faithfulness
Goodness

The degree to which these traits are manifested in the life depends upon the extent to which the Christian trusts the Lord with every detail of his life, and upon his maturity in Christ. One who is only beginning to understand the ministry of the Holy Spirit should not be discouraged if he is not as fruitful as more mature Christians who have known and experienced this truth for a longer period.

Why is it that most Christians are not experiencing the abundant life?

5

2. CARNAL CHRISTIANS CANNOT EXPERIENCE THE ABUNDANT AND FRUITFUL CHRISTIAN LIFE.

The carnal man trusts in his own efforts to live the Christian life:

A. He is either uninformed about, or has forgotten, God's love, forgiveness, and power (Romans 5:8-10; Hebrews 10:1-25; I John 1:2; 1:3; II Peter 1:9; Acts 1:8).

B. He has an up-and-down spiritual experience.

C. He cannot understand himself—he wants to do what is right, but cannot.

D. He fails to draw upon the power of the Holy Spirit to live the Christian life.

(I Corinthians 3:1-3; Romans 7:15-24; 8:7; Galatians 5:16-18)

6

THE CARNAL MAN—Some or all of the following traits may characterize the Christian who does not fully trust God:

Ignorance of his spiritual heritage
Unbelief
Disobedience
Loss of love for God and for others
Poor prayer life
No desire for Bible study

Legalistic attitude
Impure thoughts
Jealousy
Guilt
Worry
Discouragement
Critical spirit
Frustration
Aimlessness

(The individual who professes to be a Christian but who continues to practice sin should realize that he may not be a Christian at all, according to I John 2:3; 3:6,9; Ephesians 5:5).

The third truth gives us the only solution to this problem . . . 7

---

3. JESUS PROMISED THE ABUNDANT AND FRUITFUL LIFE AS THE RESULT OF BEING FILLED (DIRECTED AND EMPOWERED) BY THE HOLY SPIRIT.

The Spirit-filled life is the Christ-directed life by which Christ lives His life in and through us in the power of the Holy Spirit (John 15).

A. One becomes a Christian through the ministry of the Holy Spirit, according to John 3:1-8. From the moment of spiritual birth, the Christian is indwelt by the Holy Spirit at all times (John 1:12; Colossians 2:9, 10; John 14:16, 17). **Though all Christians are indwelt by the Holy Spirit, not all Christians are filled (directed and empowered) by the Holy Spirit.**

8

B. The Holy Spirit is the source of the overflowing life (John 7:37-39).

C. The Holy Spirit came to glorify Christ (John 16:1-15). When one is filled with the Holy Spirit, he is a true disciple of Christ.

D. In His last command before His ascension, Christ promised the power of the Holy Spirit to enable us to be witnesses for Him (Acts 1:1-9).

How, then, can one be filled with the Holy Spirit?

9

4. WE ARE FILLED (DIRECTED AND EMPOWERED) BY THE HOLY SPIRIT BY FAITH; THEN WE CAN EXPERIENCE THE ABUNDANT AND FRUITFUL LIFE WHICH CHRIST PROMISED TO EACH CHRISTIAN.

You can appropriate the filling of the Holy Spirit **right now** if you:

A. Sincerely desire to be directed and empowered by the Holy Spirit (Matthew 5:6; John 7:37-39).

B. Confess your sins.

By **faith** thank God that He **has** forgiven all of your sins — past, present and future — because Christ died for you (Colossians 2:13-15; I John 1; 2:1-3; Hebrews 10:1-17).

C. Present every area of your life to God (Romans 12:1, 2).

10

D. By **faith** claim the fullness of the Holy Spirit, according to:

1. HIS COMMAND — Be filled with the Spirit.
"And do not get drunk with wine, for that is dissipation, but be filled with the Spirit" (Ephesians 5:18).

2. HIS PROMISE — He will always answer when we pray according to His will. "And this is the confidence which we have before Him, that, if we ask anything according to His will, He hears us. And if we know that He hears us in whatever we ask, we know that we have the requests which we have asked from Him" (I John 5:14, 15).

Faith can be expressed through prayer . . .   11

HOW TO PRAY IN FAITH TO BE FILLED WITH THE HOLY SPIRIT

We are filled with the Holy Spirit by **faith** alone. However, true prayer is one way of expressing your faith. The following is a suggested prayer:

"Dear Father, I need You. I acknowledge that I have been directing my own life and that, as a result, I have sinned against You. I thank You that You have forgiven my sins through Christ's death on the cross for me. I now invite Christ to again take His place on the throne of my life. Fill me with the Holy Spirit as You **commanded** me to be filled, and as You **promised** in Your Word that You would do if I asked in faith. I pray this in the name of Jesus. As an expression of my faith, I now thank You for directing my life and for filling me with the Holy Spirit."

Does this prayer express the desire of your heart? If so, bow in prayer and trust God to fill you with the Holy Spirit **right now.**
12

HOW TO KNOW THAT YOU ARE FILLED (DIRECTED AND EMPOWERED) BY THE HOLY SPIRIT

Did you ask God to fill you with the Holy Spirit? Do you know that you are now filled with the Holy Spirit? On what authority? (On the trustworthiness of God Himself and His Word: Hebrews 11:6; Romans 14:22, 23.)

Do not depend upon feelings. The promise of God's Word, not our feelings, is our authority. The Christian lives by faith (trust) in the trustworthiness of God Himself and His Word. This train diagram illustrates the relationship between **fact** (God and His Word), **faith** (our trust in God and His Word), and **feeling** (the result of our faith and obedience) (John 14:21).

FACT   FAITH   FEELING

The train will run with or without the caboose. However, it would be futile to attempt to pull the train by the caboose. In the same way, we, as Christians, do not depend upon feelings or emotions, but we place our faith (trust) in the trustworthiness of God and the promises of His Word.
13

HOW TO WALK IN THE SPIRIT

Faith (trust in God and in His promises) is the only means by which a Christian can live the Spirit-directed life. As you continue to trust Christ moment by moment:

A. Your life will demonstrate more and more of the fruit of the Spirit (Galatians 5:22, 23) and will be more and more conformed to the image of Christ (Romans 12:2; II Corinthians 3:18).

B. Your prayer life and study of God's Word will become more meaningful.

C. You will experience His power in witnessing (Acts 1:8).

D. You will be prepared for spiritual conflict against the world (I John 2:15-17); against the flesh (Galatians 5:16, 17); and against Satan (I Peter 5:7-9; Ephesians 6:10-13).

E. You will experience His power to resist temptation and sin (I Corinthians 10:13; Philippians 4:13; Ephesians 1:19-23; 6:10; II Timothy 1:7; Romans 6:1-16).

14

IF THIS BOOKLET HAS BEEN MEANINGFUL AND HELPFUL TO YOU, PLEASE GIVE OR READ IT TO SOMEONE ELSE.

Millions of copies of this booklet, "Have You Made the Wonderful Discovery of the Spirit-filled Life?" have been distributed in most major languages around the world. As a result, thousands of Christians have learned how to experience the power and control of the Holy Spirit, moment by moment. Through the abundant life which Christ promises, and which they are now experiencing, they have become more effective in sharing their faith in Christ with others. Experience has confirmed the validity of Christ's command to the disciples to wait until they were empowered by the Holy Spirit before going forth to the world to share the good news of His love and forgiveness. Most Christians, when they have learned this truth concerning the Holy Spirit, want to be actively involved in sharing Christ and in helping to fulfill the Great Commission in our generation.

WILLIAM R. BRIGHT, President, Campus Crusade for Christ International

A special Bible study series and other helpful materials for Christian growth and witness are available from Campus Crusade.

SPIRITUAL BREATHING

By faith you can continue to experience God's love and forgiveness.

If you become aware of an area of your life (an attitude or an action) that is displeasing to the Lord, even though you are walking with Him and sincerely desiring to serve Him, simply thank God that He has forgiven your sins — past, present and future — on the basis of Christ's death on the cross. Claim His love and forgiveness by faith and continue to have fellowship with Him.

If you retake the throne of your life through sin — a definite act of disobedience — breathe spiritually.

Spiritual breathing (exhaling the impure and inhaling the pure) is an exercise in faith that enables you to continue to experience God's love and forgiveness.

1. **Exhale** — confess your sin — agree with God concerning your sin and thank Him for His forgiveness of it, according to I John 1:9 and Hebrews 10:1-25. Confession involves repentance — a change in attitude and action.

2. **Inhale** — surrender the control of your life to Christ, and appropriate (receive) the fullness of the Holy Spirit by faith. Trust that He now directs and empowers you, according to the **command** of Ephesians 5:18, and the **promise** of I John 5:14, 15.

15

addressed to fictitious people were devised by Bill Bright. "The Van Dusen Letter" was written to a prominent business acquaintance who had requested information on how to become a Christian (1959); "The Paul Brown Letter" was written to a graduate student who wanted to know more about God's will for his life and vocation (1963). In the latter, Bill discusses the "Sound-Mind Principle" (II Timothy 1:7), referring to "a well-balanced mind under the control of the Holy Spirit," by which one can really know God's will for his or her life. Both letters have been distributed widely.

Next in importance to the *Four Spiritual Laws* in Campus Crusade is another booklet, entitled *Have You Made the Wonderful Discovery of the Spirit-Filled Life?* first published in 1966 and meant to be used after conversion. This booklet, influenced by Keswick holiness themes, is designed to instruct a Christian on how to be "filled with the Spirit" and participate, thereupon, in "the abundant life." Over 50 million copies have been distributed to date.

Shortly after the *Four Spiritual Laws* and *Holy Spirit* booklets were published, Bill designed a study course, a series of ten work-books (about 500 pages in all) entitled *Ten Basic Steps Toward Christian Maturity* and first published in 1968. Meant primarily for new converts, they include separate studies of the uniqueness of Jesus; the steps themselves, covering the "Christian adventure," the abundant life, prayer, the Holy Spirit, the Bible, obedience, witnessing, stewardship; and highlights of the Old Testament and New Testament—again encompassing Bill's how-to-do-it, pragmatic methodology.

Finally, the more well known series of nine "transferable concepts" was developed by Bill in as many small booklets (again, about 500 pages altogether), meant for use in personal devotions, follow-up of new converts, and group study. A *transferable concept* may be defined as an idea or a truth that can be transferred or communicated from one person to another without distorting or diluting its original meaning. First published in 1971–1972, the transferable concepts include booklets on how to be sure you are a Christian, how to experience God's love and forgiveness, how to be filled with the Spirit, how to walk in the Spirit, how to witness in the Spirit, how to introduce others to Christ, how to help fulfill the Great Commission, how to love by faith (possibly Bill's most creative writing), and how to pray.

All of these works together with a variety of other booklets and books, including those by Bill himself and the mammoth apologetic studies by Josh McDowell, are widely read and utilized within the ministry of Campus Crusade worldwide—alongside the New American Standard Bible, the main translation used by the movement. Indeed, they are first priority evangelistic and training materials in the movement, designed to be read before any other theological works.

THE PARA-CHURCH

At this point, brief mention needs to be made about Bill Bright's feelings concerning the institutional church and its role. Obviously, though many people are unaware of this fact, Campus Crusade is not itself a church. No sacramental celebrations are allowed within any of the movement's regular gatherings. Ordained ministers on staff are trained to operate as lay people within the movement. Not a church, Campus Crusade is rather a "para-church" organization, a "companion" to the church but with somewhat different functions.

In Bill's theology, the movement may introduce people to Christ and disciple them, but these individuals are encouraged from the start to join a church and become active in its ministry and fellowship. He feels it is the church's responsibility to teach the finer points of doctrine, administer the sacraments or ordinances, and, where appropriate, take a stand on controversial issues. Campus Crusade, to use Bill's phrase, is a "servant of the church," seeking to carry out Christian responsibilities (campus evangelism, for instance) that the church is either unable or unwilling to perform. Indeed, in some of its programs (Here's Life, for example) the movement does work hand-in-hand with the church. Bill himself still is a member of Hollywood Pres., and sometimes he attends more than one service on Sunday in churches located on his travel itinerary and speaks regularly in many of them. Vonette has her membership in the First

Presbyterian Church of San Bernardino. She also frequently attends and preaches in other churches in the course of her travels. All new staff are required, within three months' time, to join and become active in a local church of their own choice. Finally, Bill has always maintained that, if the institutional church were to actually pick up and do what Campus Crusade is doing in evangelism and discipleship training, there would no longer be a need for his organization to exist. Of course, that's hardly likely now, if it ever was before.

FAITH, LOVE, AND HOLINESS

Bill Bright is a man of faith—great faith, in fact. For him, faith is another word for trust. It is not mere belief, not just intellectual assent to doctrines. Faith in God is absolutely essential for salvation in the Pauline sense, but, more than that, it is also necessary for human fulfillment in our relationships with others. Friendship and collegiality demand trust. If we want God as our friend, and if we desire to do his work in the world—to work with him—we have to trust in him and rely on him completely. "All things work together for good to them that love God, to them who are called according to his purpose" (Romans 8:28). Bill insists that "God has proven himself to be worthy of our trust. There are thousands of promises, and no Christian has ever found any of them to be untrue. When he says something, you can stake your life on it—you can know that he will not fail you." Faith in God must be so strong, so unflinching, that even when our world crumbles (as it did for Bill during the Big Thompson flash flood in 1976), we will thank God and praise him anyway. Because somehow, in a manner beyond our human understanding, all things do work together for good in the life of a man or woman of faith. Bill's faith is pragmatic; it works. Thus, the impossible doesn't just become possible, it becomes *normative*, because nothing is impossible with God. And if we trust him absolutely, nothing is impossible for us either. Bill's vision of doing the impossible—of fulfilling the Great Commission in our generation—is a result of his faith. This is why he demands that his staff raise their own support. Bill feels strongly that the process involved in that activity (a "privilege") guarantees the development of absolute trust in God on the part of an individual. Furthermore, the minimal salaries raised keep staff in that trust relationship with God and with each other, because, in order to subsist, they have to rely not only on God but also on each other. Low salary ceilings and the support-raising activity itself mean no financial security and make any desire for "independence" illusory, which is exactly what Bill wants in his extended family—sisters and brothers who trust God and each other for everything they need.

In Bill's theology, the best evidence, and controlling power, of holiness is love, an attitude of the heart ignited only by faith. For the president of Campus Crusade, there are just two kinds of Christian—carnal and spiritual. Carnal Christians are indwelt by the Holy Spirit, but they are not controlled and filled by that Spirit. Sin still manifests itself in the life of the carnal believer, primarily as self-centeredness. The carnal believer, moreover, exhibits some or all of the following traits: ignorance of his or her spiritual heritage, unbelief, disobedience, loss of love for God and for others, a poor prayer life, no desire for Bible study, legalistic attitudes, impure thoughts, jealousy, guilt, worry, discouragement, a "critical spirit," frustration, and aimlessness. But the carnal believer can be filled and empowered by the Spirit who already dwells within his or her life—by faith—by sincerely desiring to be empowered and directed by the Holy Spirit; by confession of sin; and by presenting every area of his or her life to God. The Spirit-filled life, then, is an ongoing "walk" not merely a one-time experience or feeling. The infilling of the Spirit is maintained by what Bill calls *spiritual breathing*, exhaling the impure and inhaling the pure. "If you retake the throne of your life through sin—a definite act of disobedience—breathe spiritually. Exhale—confess your sin. . . . Confession involves repentance—a change in attitude and action. Inhale—surrender the control of your life to Christ, and appropriate (receive) the fullness of the Holy Spirit by faith. Trust that he now directs and empowers you, according to the *command* of Ephesians 5:18, and the *promise* of I John 5:14, 15." And the result? Holiness, the fundamental characteristic of the spiritual Christian, exemplified by Christ-centeredness, empowerment for service, witnessing, an effective prayer life, understanding of God's Word, a trust in God, obedience to God, love, joy, peace, patience, kindness, faithfulness, and goodness in general.

After the departure from the movement of Bill's closest colleagues in the late 1960s, and in the wake of one of the greatest crises in the movement's history, Bill developed the transferable concept of "loving by faith"—for him, the most important mark of holiness. In it, he argues that Christian ideal of *agape*, self-giving love, cannot be achieved by an individual's efforts alone. That, too, must be appropriated by faith and is the natural consequence of the Spirit's infilling. "We are commanded to love God," Bill explains, "and we are commanded to love our neighbors, our enemies, and ourselves. Love for our neighbor fulfills God's love and demonstrates our relationship to him. The Holy Spirit supplies the love we need. The principle of loving by faith is based on a command and a promise. God *commands* us to love and he *promises* that he will hear and answer when we pray according to his will. God has an unending supply of *agape* from which we can draw by faith." Bill feels strongly that, "when Christians begin to act like Christians and love God, their neighbors as themselves, their enemies and especially their Christian brothers and sisters—regardless of color, race, or class—we shall see demonstrated in our time, as in the first century, a great transformation in the whole of society, in man's relationship with man. Men and women will marvel, as they did in the first century, when they observe our attitudes and actions. 'How they love one another.' " This, he insists, is the fundamental answer to the "problems of war, race, capital, and labor."

As a concrete demonstration of the principle of loving by faith and of holiness more generally, Bill Bright initiated a policy of noncriticism that operates as the first and foremost policy within Campus Crusade for Christ. As a policy, noncriticism means that staff must not criticize other churches, religious organizations, movements, and other Christians of any persuasion. In his words, the policy "grew out of a conviction that we are to live holy lives, and you can't live a holy life if you are a gossiper or a slanderer. We reason that if we allow criticism within our movement—a destructive stance, embracing a petty, jealous, or 'critical' spirit that puts people down—we are allowing our staff to become victims of a carnal influence, since criticism is a mark of the carnal Christian." And, according to the movement's campus ministry manual, "A critical attitude of fellow staff, of the Campus Crusade ministry or of other individuals or groups shall be considered as evidence of disloyalty to Christ, and shall be accepted as an act of resignation."

The essentials, then, of Bill Bright's "simple" theology are centered on faith as a matter of free choice and as an act of the will involving absolute trust in God and holiness of living, made possible by the infilling of the Holy Spirit, and characterized by the rejection of both dogmatism and legalism and by 100 percent commitment to Christ and his will. Holiness, an attitude of the heart manifested in action, means primarily loving God, one's self, one's neighbors, and one's enemies. Methodologically, this theology is carried out in relationship with the church by aggressive evangelism marked by a practical, pragmatic, how-to-do-it approach, and with the avoidance of criticism of other Christians regardless of their persuasion. When taken seriously, this theology and methodology—focused on people as God's method—is completely positive in theory, workable in practice, and ecumenical in spirit.

7 In the World but Not of It

The things commanded in the gospel are really true of the saints.
They are not only required of all men, but they are facts in the
life and experience of the saints. The saints really love their
enemies, bless them that curse them, do good to those that hate
them and pray for them that despitefully use and persecute them.

CHARLES G. FINNEY, *Systematic Theology*

In his *Institutes of the Christian Religion* ("On Christian Liberty"),
John Calvin, building on Paul, talks about how Christians should
approach material things. They are not necessarily evil in themselves
but "indifferent": "We are bound by no obligation before God
respecting external things, which in themselves are indifferent,
but ... we may indifferently sometimes use and at other times omit
them." Indeed, he warns us about becoming excessively negative
concerning worldly goods: "For when the conscience has once fallen
into the snare, it enters a long and inextricable labyrinth from which
it is afterwards difficult to escape. ... If anyone imagine a delicate
food to be unlawful, he will ere long have no tranquility before God
in eating brown bread and common viands, while he remembers that
he might support his body with meat of a quality still inferior. If he
hesitates respecting good wine, he will afterwards be unable with
any peace of conscience to drink the most vapid; and at last he will
not presume to touch purer and sweeter water than others. In short,
he will come to think it criminal to step over a twig that lies across
his path."

By *indifferent*, Calvin means that worldly things must not be
indulged in—made an idol. They must be used indifferently. Where

material things are "ardently coveted, proudly boasted, or luxurious-ly lavished, these things . . . are completely polluted." He continues: "Ivory and gold, and riches of all kinds, are certainly blessings of Divine Providence, not only permitted, but expressly designed for the use of men; nor are we anywhere prohibited to laugh or to be satiated with food, or to annex new possessions to those already enjoyed by ourselves or by our ancestors, or to be delighted with musical harmony, or to drink wine. This is indeed true; but amidst an abundance of all things, to be immersed in sensual delights, to inebriate the heart and mind with present pleasures, and perpetually to grasp new ones—these things are very remote from a legitimate use of Divine blessings." The issue, then, is idolatry. Material goods may be enjoyed, but they may not be idolized. Culture and all of its manifestations are never intrinsically bad. They are evil only when they are self-glorifying and rebellious against God.

MONEY AND MATERIAL SUCCESS

A considerable amount of money passes through Campus Crusade for Christ each year—almost $42 million in 1977. Of this amount, 66 percent was contributed for staff support, raised individually by each person; 12 percent was solicited for special projects; 17 percent was earned through sales of literature, materials, and services; 3 percent came from conference registrations (mainly at Arrowhead Springs); and 2 percent was generated from other sources. According to the December 15, 1976, listing of nonprofit organizations, Campus Crusade met the standards for charitable solicitation purposes of the Council of Better Business Bureaus. Included in this evaluation are some forty guidelines that require of each group a responsible governing body, financial accountability, ethical fund raising, and truthful advertising and information generally. Every year Campus Crusade publishes a financial report, itemizing contributions and expenditures, and attested to by certified public accountants, that is available to anyone.

Bill and Vonette Bright's Federal Income Tax return for 1976 indicates a total income of $13,857.54. This figure does not reflect their use of an automobile and house in San Bernardino. A friend loans them a car for ministry and personal use. In lieu of paying rent on their house located at Arrowhead Springs, Bill and Vonette take a salary $1,800 per year lower than what they would otherwise be eligible to receive. They are also responsible to raise a similar amount of funds to help defray some of the expenses that Campus Crusade incurs in maintaining the house. All of their honoraria and royalties are given to the ministry. And although they list their personal net worth "officially" as less than $25,000, the exact amount is, in fact, closer to $5,000.

In terms of material success, Bill, by and large, shares Calvin's thinking on the matter. Worldly goods may be enjoyed as long as they don't become an idol. He and Vonette have lived very comfortably since the beginning of Campus Crusade, in other people's homes. Bill has always oriented his ministry to being all things to all people and has wanted to live in a home where both the richest and the poorest could feel comfortable. 110 Stone Canyon Road, owned by Henrietta Mears, was meant to be such a place, and so is the beautiful home and surrounding land where Bill and Vonette live now at Arrowhead Springs, owned by Campus Crusade as an organization. It would surely rent on the open market for far more than the $150 per month charged against the couple's pay. But because of their travel schedule, both are home on the average of just a few days a month. Bill and Vonette eat well, too—at home, in the office, and on their travels. But they also fast one day each week to identify in a small way with the world's poor. And the car they drive is hardly a luxury vehicle.

Bill and Campus Crusade do have a ministry to the wealthy. From the time he was a seminary student at Hollywood Pres., the president of Campus Crusade has known rich individuals who were and are committed Christians. He says, "Some of the most effective men and women I know are wealthy. They lead more people to Christ, they give generously of their funds, and are less 'worldly' than some I know who really don't have anything. We believe that if a person walks with God, he or she will obey God, and will do whatever God commands."

One concrete way in which Campus Crusade ministers to the
wealthy is through its executive seminars, held mostly at Arrowhead
Springs, but also in other places around the world. Business executives attend *gratis* these gatherings, where they are dined but not
wined in a fine manner. The "spread" at exective seminars is as good
as that to be found in many corporate dining rooms. The fact that
there are no ashtrays and no "No Smoking" signs in the hotel at
Arrowhead Springs suprises a number of the visiting business people,
some of whom do smoke outside and in their private rooms. Again,
Bill does not like to put people down, even though smoking is not
condoned at Arrowhead Springs. What Bill does share with the
wealthy is that they should be generous, especially if they are
Christians. And he has been known to "suggest" the same thing to
these people that Jesus demanded of the rich young ruler, without
too much in the way of results. However, many business people—
new converts and mature believers alike—do give generously to the
work of Campus Crusade after the close of the seminars, some
sacrificially.

Bill's greatest concern is that rich Christians, in their personal
devotion and stewardship, resist the temptation to idolatry. Bill and
Vonette do live well, but they do not make their comforts an idol.
The fact is that the Brights live about as well as the typical middle-
class pastor of a medium-sized Protestant church in the United
States, with a very nice parsonage, and far less well than most
Protestant leaders of their stature and eminence, including Oral
Roberts and Billy Graham. And their income is nothing compared to
that of the average corporate executive who presides over a staff of
more than 6,500. Finally, just about anyone who really examines the
material gains of Bill and Vonette and the financial operation of
Campus Crusade trying to find unethical uses of funds will surely be
very disappointed.

THE MEDIA AND MADISON AVENUE

Bill Bright the pragmatist has for many years utilized both the
mass media in general and Madison Avenue advertising techniques

in particular to get the gospel as he understands it across to as many people as possible. He is well aware that advertising is most often employed in a worldly manner. It fosters cynicism, because goods offered through advertising usually aren't as wonderful as they are made out to be, and advertising, which strengthens free-enterprise competition and the capitalistic economic system, does call upon individuals, and tempts them, to purchase things they really don't need. Yet advertising through the mass media reaches almost everyone, and it is an integral part of the American way of life. So Bill feels free to utilize it on a massive scale—as in the I found it! campaign—to confront people with the gospel in terms they can best understand. Although media advertising often does deceive, Bill attempts to transform the technique by offering a message that, as far as he's concerned, is both completely true and absolutely necessary. Instead of rejecting a successful secular technique, he utilizes it in order to make it serve God and God's purpose for the world—a very Calvinistic and pragmatic approach, to say the least.

At first, Bill was skeptical about employing a gimmick to evangelize the world. Before the *Four Spiritual Laws,* however, a noted businessman pointed out to him that, in his witnessing, he probably said essentially the same thing during each personal encounter, so why not write it down and duplicate it, as a "spiritual pitch," for others in order to standardize the approach and teach it easily? Out of this advice came *God's Plan for Your Life* and, later, the *Four Spiritual Laws* booklet. The use of the mass media and Madison Avenue proved itself to Bill because, in his judgment, it worked. Vast numbers of individuals responded to the gospel message presented in that way, indicated to Campus Crusade that they had done so, and began sharing it with others. So Bill was satisfied.

The president of Campus Crusade for Christ had discerned the use of mass communications already in Scripture. "When God chose to give His laws to the nation of Israel," he relates, "He chose a mass communications technique by writing the laws on stone tablets for Moses to show the people. The prophet Habakkuk, who was given a vision from God, was told, 'Write my answer on a billboard, large and clear, so that anyone can read it at a glance and rush to tell the others' (Habakkuk 2:2, Living Bible). The Apostle Paul and other early leaders of the Church wrote letters to groups of believers in local churches throughout the then known world. Some of those letters are, of course, now contained within the New Testament. Jesus also used mass communications methods and techniques to convey the truth to the masses. He quoted from the Old Testament, thus multiplying God's original communication. He spoke often in parables, thus dramatizing practical principles to heighten their retention by the listeners. He spoke to large masses of people, many times performing miracles to get their attention—as illustrated by his multiplying of the loaves and fishes. Perhaps the best illustration of God's use of the mass media lies in the Bible itself. The Bible has been published in more translations and in more languages and in greater quantities by far than any other book in history. God enabled his children to utilize the medium of the printed page to multiply his Word so that hundreds of millions upon millions of people might come to know him in a personal way through his Son."

Bill goes on to say, "At Campus Crusade, we see mass media tools as having three uses: for evangelism, discipleship training, and motivation. In the Here's Life, America movement, we incorporated all the practical, available communications tools into a total strategy for the saturation of cities with the I found it! message." For this campaign in the United States and other developed countries, billboards, bumper stickers, buttons, and telephone numbers were used. But to reach the 62 percent of the world living in villages and rural areas, many of them illiterate, Here's Life, World, has been modified to the rural setting. Bill explains: "Where there are not sufficient Christians to support Here's Life programs, mobile circuit-riding vans and motorcycles will penetrate remote places, setting up outdoor theater showings of films and also distributing literature and recordings. I can envision the development of a new kind of TV receiving set—large-screen, battery- or solar-powered, durable—which could be placed in hundreds of thousands of villages."

Speaking of his use of media tools for evangelism more generally, Bill cites the fact that in "every television special there is more than one opportunity for the viewer to receive Christ. Invitations to

receive Christ are given during the half-time program of our
televised Athletes in Action basketball games. We have a progressive
program for producing evangelistic films, books, cassettes, publications, and literature." Campus Crusade publishes many study materials for its worldwide program of discipleship training as well. "We
also utilize mass communications to *motivate* Christians to become
disciples and to become involved in God's work, to become part of
his solution for the world, to live godly lives and to share Christ as a
way of life."

Bill feels strongly that, in using the mass media and Madison
Avenue, Campus Crusade depends on the Holy Spirit to compel
individuals to respond. "We don't apologize for using media. I
believe that if the Lord Jesus Christ were here today, he would
employ every possible means of getting his message to the masses.
And that's what we're trying to do. It is not enough to proclaim the
message through radio, television, newspapers, and billboards. It is
God the Holy Spirit who takes the message and applies it to the
hearts of the viewers, listeners, and readers and transforms their lives
in the process." And Bright reminds his critics that, "for every hour
of evangelism, we probably spend a dozen or a hundred hours in
teaching Christians how to grow and mature."

WOMEN IN THE MOVEMENT

In order to understand the role of women in Campus Crusade, and
the theological and sociological underpinnings of that role, we have
to start with Vonette Zachary Bright. Early in her marriage to Bill,
Vonette was influenced by one of their neighbors, Emmeline Pankhurst, who had been active in the woman-suffrage movement in
England. Vonette explains: "It was her opinion that because of my
training and education, I was far too intelligent to spend time
washing windows, sweeping patios, and doing things which did not
have to be done. She bluntly told me that my successful husband
should pay to have these things done so that I could spend my time
on more challenging and profitable pursuits.

"I chuckled at her advice for I was thrilled to have my own home

and to be Bill Bright's wife, but at the same time I found myself
going the long way about doing tasks because I wanted to keep busy
until Bill got home. Many times I walked from our little house at the
top of a hill above Hollywood Boulevard down to a store on the
boulevard and back, about a three-mile distance, in order to fill the
hours.

"As the months passed and Miss Pankhurst continued to instruct
me in the ills of housewifery, it began to make an impression. I soon
began to question whether or not being domestically involved was
really satisfying. As a young girl, I had done enough domestic tasks at
home to realize that there was not fulfillment for a lifetime in just
doing housework."

Soon after that, Vonette received an offer to teach in the Los
Angeles school system. She also enrolled in graduate school at the
University of Southern California, where she developed a teaching
methodology that was later used within Campus Crusade. Vonette's
public school teaching career ended in 1951, when she co-founded
Campus Crusade at UCLA and directed its ministry on campus
during Bill's increasing travels away from Westwood—teaching and
training both women and men. But from the beginning, Vonette
emphasized working with women in her ministry.

Throughout the history of the movement, Vonette has been a vital
force, sharing in Bill's ministry by developing her own, serving as the
only woman on the board of directors and in the cabinet, and
advising Bill personally. She now travels almost everywhere with her
husband and has her own speaking engagements. The focus of her
ministry, though, is the Great Commission Prayer Crusade, of which
she is director, a movement within Campus Crusade that has a
mailing list of 35,000 people who receive its "Prayer and Praise
Reminder" each month. "We've also developed prayer workshops in
conjunction with the Here's Life movements," Vonette says. "We
have sponsored prayer crusades and a national prayer congress. The
most recent development here is the Prayer/Care Ministry. I began
to think, why should prayer always be a voluntary activity? Then
God impressed me with the idea of supporting people to pray as part
of our ministry. I shared this idea with Bill and some of the other

leaders in our movement. They agreed with me, and so we began to recruit staff to come and spend their time in prayer." Of course, since that first twenty-four-hour prayer chain at UCLA in 1951, intercessory prayer has been one of the most important features of Campus Crusade, an organized and methodical activity, even though prayer ministry has been a traditional role of women in the church.

Today, Vonette also sits on a committee established at the 1974 Lausanne International Congress on World Evangelization to continue the congress' work of coordinating efforts of individuals, churches, and other organizations to reach the world with the gospel. Leighton Ford, Billy Graham's progressive brother-in-law and heir apparent, chairs the committee, and Vonette Zachary Bright is one of the only female members.

Vonette is as exuberant as Bill is reserved. Both she and her husband are lay members of The United Presbyterian Church in the U.S.A., a denomination that ordains women both as ruling elders and as pastors. And both of them support the ordination of women. (One of Vonette's favorite parish ministries is that of a couple where the husband does most of the administrative work and the wife preaches.) Bill admits that, as far as he is concerned, though it is not likely, a woman could succeed him as president of the organization. Vonette explains: "Women have a very active role in this ministry. They receive the same training as men. There are no limitations put on the women." Such is the ideal, but what is the actual practice?

Many outsiders and some insiders will notice an apparent contradiction in the movement with respect to the role of women. This contradiction is real and is basically a reflection of the struggle in Bill's thinking between his idealism and his pragmatism. Ideally, he believes women should be able to do anything men can do in Campus Crusade and in the church as well. But will it *work?* Both Bill and Vonette want to be all things to all people. Yet they are still victims—if that is an appropriate word—of social convention. The Brights think that if women in leadership even *seem* to challenge men's authority, they will lose both the respect and the following of men. Thus the traditional "feminine" role is dominant in instructions to staff in the campus ministry manual, for instance, which states

clearly: "A woman in a place of leadership should not try to compete
with the men of the organization on a man-to-man basis. In attempting to do so, she may antagonize the man and trample his pride, and
even appear to threaten his position. She may tend to become
dictatorial and irritating. Such a situation will lead to the inevitable
defeat of the whole ministry or program. A woman must remember
that she is a woman and do all that she can to keep every attribute
that is associated with womanhood."

Vonette thinks it best for women to retain their "femininity"
(small wonder, then, that Marabel Morgan—*The Total Woman*—is
a former Campus Crusade staffer) and both Bill and Vonette are
keenly aware that most women on staff come from very traditional
family or church backgrounds and find it a radical step, in many
instances, to join staff and work in ministry of any kind sixty hours
per week. They may find it difficult to explain to parents and friends
who still see woman's role in the home alone, and certainly not in the
active ministry, even if she is unmarried. Furthermore, the movement has within its ranks a number of campus directors of ministry
and middle management men trained in very conservative seminaries that don't even admit women to their ministerial programs, who
don't believe that women should teach the Bible to men or have
authority over them in any way. These men tend to interpret Bill's
pragmatic statements on the role of women theologically, thus giving
them even more authority. And Bill does not wish to offend them.
Finally, in Vonette's words, "Too many people today stereotype
Christianity as a sign of weakness—saying it is something only for
women. They say you can't really be a man and be a Christian. I feel
that to have a woman in the position of leadership [as president of
Campus Crusade, for example] would only tend to enforce that
viewpoint." Again, neither Bill nor Vonette have any theological or
biblical objections to an equal role for women in Campus Crusade or
in the church, though Vonette always makes it clear when she
preaches that she is doing so under her husband's authority, which
makes her preaching tolerable to many conservatives on the same
issue who support the movement.

In the U.S. campus ministry—in the field—women rarely have
any authority over men and do not usually teach men in the follow-

up and discipling process. No woman in the United States has the title of director of ministry on campus, except in women's colleges; nor are any of them area directors, and so on up the bureaucratic ladder. But this is not the case so much elsewhere in the movement, particularly in Europe, where social convention in a good number of countries does not work to prevent women from entering the ministry. The movement's one woman director of campus ministry on a coed campus works at the University of Uppsala, Sweden, probably one of the most "liberal" university communities in the democratic world. Furthermore, the international *Agape* movement, in which most of the staff are women, allows women to teach and train men on a regular basis. So we can see that the issue is cultural not theological.

At headquarters, women appear to have a more egalitarian role. Marilyn Henderson, one of the Big Thompson flash flood survivors, heads all U.S. women's work and, by virtue of that office, has a good deal of influence in the movement. Judy Downs Douglass, a staff member since 1964 and editor of *Worldwide Challenge*, Campus Crusade's monthly magazine, is also a prominent staff member who has men reporting to her. She considers herself a moderate feminist and would love to see more women in prominent leadership positions within the movement, though she feels that this must happen gradually to avoid the shock and offense that would otherwise probably be unavoidable. Judy and a handful of other staff women attend meetings of the newly formed Evangelical Women's Caucus, which seeks to promote within the American evangelical movement as a whole biblical feminism, a kind of feminist thinking that will allow both single and married Christian women who are committed to the authority of Scripture to find God's will for their lives—as their own persons—and grow in their calling, even if it means the ordained ministry.

SOCIAL CONCERNS: THE AGAPE PERSON

The issue of the role of women in Campus Crusade today leads logically to the topic of social concern within the movement. Does the gospel have anything to say about Christian obligations to better

the conditions and structures of society that often oppress both men
and women? What about social and economic injustice? Racism?
Religious persecution? Political involvement? In 1974, at the Lausanne International Congress on World Evangelization convened by
Billy Graham, Bill Bright was one of the architects of the Lausanne
Covenant, which affirms and describes the Christian mandate for
world evangelism and defines the scope of Christian social responsibility as follows:

> We affirm that God is both the Creator and the Judge of all men. We
> therefore should share his concern for justice and reconciliation through-
> out human society and for the liberation of men from every kind of
> oppression. Because mankind is made in the image of God, every person,
> regardless of race, religion, colour, culture, class, sex or age, has an
> intrinsic dignity because of which he should be respected and served, not
> exploited. Here too we express penitence both for our own neglect and for
> having sometimes regarded evangelism and social concern as mutually
> exclusive. Although reconciliation with man is not reconciliation with
> God, nor is social action evangelism, nor is political liberation salvation,
> nevertheless we affirm that evangelism and socio-political involvement
> are both part of our Christian duty. For both are necessary expressions of
> our doctrines of God and man, our love for our neighbour and our
> obedience to Jesus Christ. The message of salvation implies also a message
> of judgment upon every form of alienation, oppression and discrimination,
> and we should not be afraid to denounce evil and injustice wherever they
> exist. When people receive Christ they are born again into his kingdom
> and must seek not only to exhibit but also to spread its righteousness in the
> midst of an unrighteous world. The salvation we claim should be trans-
> forming as in the totality of our personal and social responsibilities. Faith
> without works is dead.

On the matter of human rights and freedom from religious and
political persecution in particular, the Lausanne Covenant is also
clear:

> It is the God-appointed duty of every government to secure conditions
> of peace, justice and liberty in which the church may obey God, serve the
> Lord Christ, and preach the gospel without interference. We therefore
> pray for the leaders of the nations and call upon them to guarantee
> freedom of thought and conscience, and freedom to practice and propa-
> gate religion in accordance with the will of God and as set forth in the

Universal Declaration of Human Rights. We also express our deep concern for all who have been unjustly imprisoned, and especially for our brethren who are suffering for their testimony to the Lord Jesus. We promise to pray and work for their freedom. At the same time we refuse to be intimidated by their fate. God helping us, we too will seek to stand against injustice and to remain faithful to the gospel, whatever the cost. We do not forget the warnings of Jesus that persecution is inevitable.

Campus Crusade has for many years been accused of neglecting the social dimension of the gospel as outlined in the Lausanne Covenant. But Bill insists, "I have always been socially concerned." Indeed, as mentioned before, he spent five years and considerable time each week leading the deputation work at Hollywood Pres. in the skid row rescue missions and jails of Los Angeles. Then, just before the birth of Campus Crusade, Bill and Vonette drew up a covenant renouncing all their materialistic ambitions and promising to live by faith. If the fight against materialism is part of Christian social concern—and it is—then Bill Bright can be given credit for joining that struggle.

Campus Crusade staff have also been engaged in evangelism, discipleship training, and community involvement in ghetto areas of such American cities as Miami, Newark, New York, Chicago, and Los Angeles, translating the gospel message as they understand it into the language of thought and action characterizing these inner-city minority communities. Furthermore, over the years Bill has developed a number of largely social ministries within the movement, geared to the specific needs of oppressed people; including work with prisoners; an intercultural ministry focusing on racial and ethnic minorities; a ministry to international students, many of whom are studying in the United States from Third World countries; and, most important perhaps, the *Agape* movement, a Christian service corps modeled after the Peace Corps.

In addition, Bill has put together a five-point strategy for U.S. Christians to become politically concerned and involved, though Campus Crusade staff members themselves are required to refrain from active political involvement for the sake of being all things to all people, even those on the "other side" of the political spectrum. The duties Bright feels Christians should embrace in this country include (1) prayer; (2) registering to vote; (3) becoming informed; (4) helping to elect "godly" people—not necessarily Christians alone—marked by integrity, industriousness, biblical guidance, a concern for and practice of justice, demonstrated capability, and godliness in general; and (5) voting when the day arrives. Godly candidates may be of any party, any race, and either sex.

But when all is said and done, Campus Crusade for Christ as a whole, like other evangelical organizations, has not given social concern the primacy demanded by the Lausanne Covenant. Many, if not most, of its staff still question the priority of Christian social responsibility in their own ministries and in the ministry of the movement in general. So Bill has begun to strengthen the social witness of Campus Crusade by insisting that most Americans seeking to serve anywhere outside the United States experience cross-cultural training. And, responding to the concerns of his own black staff members and black pastors involved in the movement, he is recruiting more black personnel and developing new black ministries to be directed by black leaders. With the encouragement of Campus Crusade's Latin American director, Sergio Garcia Romo, Bill and his staff have put together a strong social action component as part of the new standardized international training curriculum—"building the *agape* person"—that all of the movement's staff will study. Garcia himself requires all of his staff members, before beginning work, to go through a "rural plunge" into Latin American rural poverty areas for a few weeks with very little money. They are told to make their own way in order to learn first-hand what it's like to live in poverty with the poor.

Bill's philosophy of "the world," of relating to human culture, derives from his theology centered on God's love for the world and his wonderful plan for those who will accept it. The world is sinful and unrighteous, but sin in individuals and in social structures can be suppressed by Spirit-filled believers who exhibit a selfless attitude and *agape* love in all their dealings with people and society. The more individuals who are won, built, and sent for Christ—and are controlled and transformed by the Spirit of holiness—the more human society will itself be transformed, until the end when God consummates his Kingdom in perfect righteousness and peace.

PART IV
MISSION

8 Campus Crusade's Ministries Today (I): The Gospel in an American Context

We are born helpless. As soon as we are fully conscious we discover loneliness. . . .

Our whole being by its very nature is one vast need; incomplete, preparatory, empty yet cluttered, crying out for Him who can untie things that are now knotted together and tie up things that are still dangling loose.

C. S. LEWIS, *The Four Loves*

CAPTURING THE CAMPUS

Among the many ministries of Campus Crusade for Christ, the campus ministry is the oldest, the largest, the best known, and the most important, because this is where most future staff members for all the ministries are recruited. Campus chapters range in size from 25 or 30 to 450 students participating in small discipleship training groups at Pennsylvania State University. Campus staff altogether communicated the gospel in one-to-one situations to nearly 150,000 people in 1976–1977. Some 8,600 individuals indicated that they received Christ during these encounters, and an additional 10,000 people prayed to receive Christ with students whom the 1,473 campus staff members had trained.

An outgrowth of the campus ministry is the summer projects program, in which more than 1,000 students participated in 1977. That summer, twenty-one projects were held in a variety of settings,

including resort areas, national parks, campgrounds, and the inner
city. Students involved take a standard summer job and spend their
free time being trained by staff members—a worker-priest ministry,
as it is sometimes called. In 1977, students working in the summer
projects shared Christ with 55,000 people, nearly 5,000 of whom
responded to the gospel affirmatively.

On campus and elsewhere, Campus Crusade focuses its community life on programs and small groups. These small groups and
programs provide the fellowship and identity that attract many
students, but, as the campus ministry manual suggests, "It is not our
purpose just to set up a program. . . . Our perspective should be to
capture the campus. The only reason for meetings is to help capture
the campus. We're not called just to teach the Christians or get a
group together. One of the temptations is to find your security in the
group of people with whom you work." The fellowship within
Campus Crusade's discipleship training groups on campus is indeed
attractive and intense, yet the groups are there not only for fellowship but to train individuals in evangelism—aggressive evangelism—
which involves "the physical (going to people), the verbal (clearly
sharing the message of Christ), and the volitional (seeking to evoke a
willful response or decision concerning what has been communicated)."

Capturing the campus is undertaken with a four-phase strategy.
Phase I is *penetration,* in which staff begin to gather students with
leadership potential (those with "a heart for God and a teachable
attitude"). The goal is usually to establish a twenty-five to forty
person nucleus of potential leaders for ministry. *Concentration* is
Phase II. Here staff and student leaders saturate one segment of the
campus—most often the freshman class—with the gospel in order to
effectively raise up the student leadership capable of executing
Phase III, which is *saturation* of the total campus community. Phase
IV, *continuation,* maintains saturation continually—"keeping Jesus
Christ before the entire campus as a live issue requiring a personal
decision." During Phase IV, Phases I, II, and III are also in full
operation simultaneously, and this is the ultimate goal by which
winning, building, and sending men and women take on a permanent, nonstop character.

A stereotype of evangelism in a difficult situation is illustrated by Crusade staff cartoonist Steve Becker.

Saturation is a key Campus Crusade strategy for evangelism and discipleship training, illustrated most visibly, perhaps, by the Berkeley blitz of 1967 and the Here's Life programs. Saturation as a concept is based on the Great Commission: preaching the gospel to every man and woman, and making disciples of all nations. In order to help staff decide whether and when a campus has been saturated with the gospel, the movement leaders have set down a number of guidelines. First, they feel that saturation has indeed occurred when 70 percent of the students have heard the gospel and have been given a chance to receive Christ, over a two-year period. Staff should be able to calculate the approximate percentage involved from their records of the number of students who have heard the gospel in meetings, through personal staff contacts, and by means of other students. Faculty and administration are included here, too. This is the "winning" aspect of campus saturation.

But saturation doesn't just involve winning; it also embraces building and sending. The guidelines suggest that at least 1 percent of the student body on a given campus should be participating in discipleship training action groups. By that, Campus Crusade means that 1 percent of a campus student body have been discipled to the point that they are witnessing at least once a week. These individuals, then, are responsible for reaching the 30 percent of the campus not initially accounted for and for contacting the incoming freshmen the following academic year.

Finally, the organization issues guidelines suggesting that at least 40 percent of discipled graduating seniors should be planning to enter some kind of full-time Christian ministry, the focus being on Campus Crusade staff. Thus the movement is assured of a continual replenishment of new staff in the wake of a high degree of transience within the organization.

Saturation of a campus with the gospel is evidenced further when staff and students can't find anyone who hasn't heard the Four Spiritual Laws; when every segment of the campus has been contacted, including blacks and other ethnic and racial minorities, internationals, faculty, and athletes; and when the results of surveys show that most of the students know how to become a Christian.

As a whole, Campus Crusade for Christ has worked most successfully on large state university campuses and within private colleges and universities with a preponderance of athletes and fraternity and sorority members—UCLA, USC, the University of Minnesota, and Penn State, for example. It has probably been least effective on high-prestige, intellectually oriented private universities and colleges, such as Harvard, Yale, and Stanford, where the more cerebral, student-directed (rather than staff-directed) Inter-Varsity Christian Fellowship tends to dominate the Christian campus ministry.

TWO STRONG CRUSADERS

Closely associated with the movement's campus ministry is Josh McDowell, traveling representative for Campus Crusade, now based in Dallas and the movement's most visible intellectual. McDowell has spoken to an estimated 5 million people on over 540 campuses in more than fifty countries over a twelve-year period. Josh speaks without notes in English and in Spanish and reads an average of 350 books per year. As a student, he drove himself so hard that he'd sometimes have to stay in bed for two weeks at a time.

McDowell spends about ninety hours of preparation on each speech he delivers, focusing either on Christian apologetics, the thrust of his best-selling book, *Evidence that Demands a Verdict,* or on "maximum sex," human sexuality from a Christian perspective.

Josh was brought up on a farm near Battle Creek, Michigan, where he milked cows twice a day in his youth and lettered in four sports, participated in student government, and acted in high school dramatics. His father, Josh concedes, was an alcoholic and "epitomized everything I hated." But after Josh became a Christian in 1959, he and his father were reconciled; the elder McDowell also received Christ shortly afterward.

Early in his Christian experience, Josh McDowell became involved with Campus Crusade. He graduated from Wheaton College in Illinois, where he studied business and economics, intending to enter law school after graduation. However, Josh made the decision to go into the ministry while still in college, and he enrolled at Talbot Theological Seminary in La Mirada, California, instead. Then he joined Campus Crusade staff and was first assigned to California State University at Fullerton. After that, he went on to the University of Washington, served as director of the ministry in Vancouver, British Columbia, assisted Hal Lindsey at UCLA, and then moved on to South America before returning to the United States.

As a bright young staff member, McDowell was asked while in Canada to direct the summer staff at Arrowhead Springs rather than serve as an instructor at the summer Institute of Biblical Studies, an assignment he had hoped for and would have much preferred. Help was short at Arrowhead Springs, and so Josh spent a great deal of time cleaning rugs, floors, and toilets—hardly an intellectual job— and he often seethed over the "indignity" of his assignment. But he remembered Jesus' washing the feet of his disciples, and he seemed to be telling him, "If I could wash their feet, why can't you scrub their floors?" That changed Josh's attitude completely.

While living in South America, McDowell recalls the time when "our movement got so big it even disturbed the fascist groups, which were very strong in Argentina at that time." Once three fascist student leaders outlined their political strategy to Josh, asking him to travel on their behalf. When he refused, one of them said, "Mister, you'd better do it, or you won't live three months to tell about it." With that, Josh launched into a discussion about Christ with them. He heard later that two of the three had become Christians and were forced to leave the country. McDowell has also had trouble in the United States. Once at Cal State, Fullerton police found twenty-four sticks of dynamite buried near the area where he was to speak. Nevertheless, Josh has remained undaunted in his ministry.

While lecturing at the University of Texas in 1970, McDowell met a woman who was also a Campus Crusade staff member. He and Dottie were married six months later and now have two children. Josh spends very little time sleeping, works too hard (like most Campus Crusade staff), and readily admits his own shortcomings. Aggressive in interpersonal relations, he has to be careful not to offend others. "Some of my big problems," he confesses, "concern being impatient with people and not being sensitive." McDowell has had a great deal of success in his own ministry on campus with white students but not with blacks, which is why the movement is presently training an American black man to take Christian apologetics to the black college and university students Josh McDowell has tried to reach but can't.

Another person associated with Campus Crusade's campus ministry is André Kole, one of America's leading illusionists and a special representative of the movement. He spends 60 percent of each year on tour and has performed in person in many countries around the world; his films have been viewed worldwide as well. Kole focuses his attention largely on college and university audiences.

André Kole's love for magic began at the age of seven, when he watched a performance of Maxo the magician in Mesa, Arizona, where both of them were living. After that, André literally lived for magic morning, noon, and night, practicing how to pick locks; hypnotizing birds, snakes, and people; and developing his ability in legerdemain. By the age of twelve, he had entertained Boy Scout groups and civic clubs in more than a dozen states and in Canada and Central America.

Upon graduation from high school, Kole began practicing his magic ten to twelve hours a day. "I remember going to bed many nights with aching fingers covered with blisters just from the manipulation of cards and other objects that I use in my shows," he declares. "My best friends in high school and college were magicians, my girlfriend was my assistant, and magic was my favorite pastime."

André developed his own tricks and illusions from the start. In one year alone, he invented more than 1,000 magical effects. Even now, he creates three or four in a week, believing that, "in order to have some successes, you have to have many failures." Kole graduated in psychology from Arizona State University, "since they didn't offer any courses in magic." By the age of twenty-five, he was married, had a family, and was a success both in magic and in business (as director of statewide operations of one of the largest corporations in Arizona). André was also co-owner of a ranch and a number of buildings and directed several enterprises in show business.

As Kole traveled, he met a group of Christians whose lives really impressed him. Nevertheless, he states, "At that time I took great pride in my reputation as a magician. I have never been fooled by any other magician, and I had no intention of being deceived by any first-century trickster—if this was all that Jesus really was." Finally, however, he gave in and became a Christian, because he was certain that Jesus was not merely a magician. Soon afterward, André spent two days with the director of Campus Crusade at Arizona State, talking with students about Christ. "I saw a response and a need that challenged me to let God really use my life." His consuming interest in fantasy and illusion completely vanished, and he was convinced at the time that he would never do magic again. That stance lasted only briefly, however, and Kole soon developed a presentation to illustrate the Four Spiritual Laws by magic. The show totally "turned off" the Campus Crusade staff who watched the first showing, but Bill Bright encouraged him, and in 1963 André and his wife Aljeana joined staff together.

Those who have seen André live, on television, or in one of his films, will remember a warm, friendly smile, piercing blue eyes, and a handsome man elegantly outfitted in white satin brocade with rhinestone buttons—a man who provokes both intense laughter and incredible suspense during his performances. Intrigue and fantasy, however, are just his means to share his faith with others. Midway through each performance, the tricks of an illusionist become André's method of sharing in his confidence in a spiritual relationship rather than rituals, in prayer rather than strange rappings and eerie whispers. "I've always felt that God is likely to use those whom the world considers most unlikely. After all," Kole says, "if God can use a magician to accomplish his purpose, he can use anybody."

But despite André's years of success both before and after his conversion, all has not been a bed of roses for him and his family. In 1976, Aljeana Kole died tragically of a brain tumor, two full years after her terminal condition was diagnosed. Though she suffered greatly and others had to care for her every need, André remembers, "never once did I hear her complain. On the contrary, many times she would say, 'Thank You Lord, for the pain.'" When she died finally, her husband and family, in the midst of their tears and sorrow, planned a special memorial service of thanksgiving and praise for Aljeana's life here and for her new life with Christ. In the same spirit that pervaded the community of Campus Crusade staff after the Big Thompson flash flood disaster, the family decided to thank God even when their whole world had crumbled. They sent out printed invitations to the service on which Aljeana and André had agreed. André explains, "We did not want the slow, depressing organ music usually associated with a funeral. When a person goes to heaven, it is the time of her coronation and the music should be in keeping with the celebration. So we had the Great Commission Company singers and orchestra provide special numbers." He concludes that, "if Aljeana is with Jesus, and Jesus is with me, then Aljeana cannot be far away." And André Kole's ministry goes on.

THE HIGH SCHOOL MINISTRY

Campus Crusade's high school ministry is less well known than its campus ministry, and it has taken a relatively low profile. A major focus of that ministry, moreover, is on training youth pastors and church lay leaders to minister effectively to high school–age young people. Plans call for more than 210 high school staff to maintain model youth ministries in fifty cities in the United States. Begun in 1966, the high school ministry motivates its staff to spend time meeting students right on the high school campus, before and after school and during lunch. They work closely with the administration in each school, adjusting their outreach to the schedules and lifestyles of the students themselves.

Just as in the movement's campus ministry, the high school staff try to win school leaders for Christ—student body presidents, class officers, team captains, and school paper editors—because, even more than on the college or university campus, high schoolers live in an environment where following the crowd and being "in" are extremely important. Furthermore, Campus Crusade knows that many high school leaders will also become leaders in college and will influence students there as well.

Staff members across the country contact students through various kinds of group meetings as well as individually. Through team meetings, staff present the gospel to teams, cheerleaders, and service clubs after school. Informal parties give staff the opportunity to interact with the students in small groups by combining fun with evangelism. School assemblies and citywide gatherings provide larger opportunities to present Christ to hundreds of students at once. Student Life meetings are evangelistic in nature and are held in a student's home every other week, with a speaker, sharing (testimonies), and singing. On occasion, school officials invite the staff to conduct a schoolwide assembly that students can attend on a voluntary basis. A "classic," finally, provides maximum outreach through a major citywide effort built around a key speaker such as André Kole.

As in the campus ministry, high school converts are discipled in small groups. Most Bible studies are also held in students' homes, and the high school staff themselves are frequently called upon to counsel with parents and their children. Furthermore, the movement's high school ministry staff work closely with local churches, their pastors, youth ministers, and lay leaders; both students and their parents are encouraged to attend these churches with their friends.

MUSIC

The music ministry of Campus Crusade for Christ began in 1966 with a vocal and instrumental group called The New Folk. Those were the days when everyone on the campus scene was "grooving" on Peter, Paul and Mary, the Beach Boys (who proudly proclaimed, "I Get Around"), and the Mamas and Papas (who were engrossed with "California Dreamin' "). The idiom was folk rock, and Campus Crusade saw it as a good vehicle to share the gospel with young people.

It all started when, in 1964, a group of college students involved with the movement attended a weekend retreat in Mound, Minnesota. The students got out their guitars and ukuleles, and began to play and sing together. "We had no intention of it going any farther than singing at the retreat," declared one of the group's members. "But the first thing we knew, we could have sung every night if we wanted to." So the music continued, and for the next two years the group performed throughout Minnesota and neighboring states. Then Bill Bright invited them to travel as part of the Campus Crusade ministry, singing secular music in a secular situation to present Christ to a secular audience. Another member of the group recalls, "We sang songs that got people to think and that would act as a bridge. Then we presented Christ in the final fifteen minutes, asking people to consider receiving him." The first year, the New Folk not only performed before 250,000 people (mostly of college and high school age) in twenty-seven states, they also won a Grammy award for their folksy "On Campus" album. The idea soon caught on, and by the second year of their touring, they "found Christian groups all over the place were doing our kind of music." In fact, The New Folk were probably the foremost predecessor of the many gospel folk and rock groups that emerged out of the Jesus movement in the late 1960s and early 1970s.

As the years passed and different types of music came into vogue, the music ministry of Campus Crusade diversified as well, not only with respect to the nature of the music but also in the style of the performers. New groups have been formed with new personnel—the

Great Commission Company, for example—and there are now separate groups in Europe and Asia also. Today the movement's music ministry has a total staff of 170.

The emergence of a variety of new instrumental and vocal groups with different musical approaches has allowed each to focus on a particular geographical area, giving the performers an opportunity to personally follow up at least some of the people they win for Christ rather than placing the whole burden of follow up in the hands of local individuals involved with Campus Crusade.

COMMUNICATIONS

The mass media ministry of Campus Crusade, of course, is an extremely important part of the work of the movement as a whole. Its rationale for existence is best described by the following statement written by the ministry staff: "We need little reminder of the powerful influence wielded by today's mass media as they glorify violence, immorality, relativity of values and irresponsibility. If we, as Christians, believe that Jesus Christ is the only hope for our troubled world, our responsibility lies in using the mass media influence as a positive force—to bring the message of Jesus Christ to millions of men and women."

The publications department, whose work is supervised by a publications committee of top movement personnel, produces the promotional materials for Campus Crusade, including *Worldwide Challenge*, a monthly magazine with a circulation of 100,000. Publications staff also write for *The Bright Side*, a monthly house organ, as well as for other periodicals used in campus and classroom evangelism. The media relations department gives information on the movement to the secular and religious press and sets up media interviews for Bill and Vonette. Creative Studios enlists graphic artists, writers, and photographers to develop full-scale advertising and public relations campaigns; to create brochures, ads, fliers, and copy for radio spots and point-of-purchase displays; and to produce visual materials for training seminars.

The print shop at Arrowhead Springs prints the organization's evangelistic materials, the shop's highest priority. The shop also produces other Campus Crusade literature, including books, manuals, and motivational materials. Some 50,000 impressions roll off the print shop's offset presses per day, meeting about 10 percent of the movement's total printing needs. Complete darkroom and bindery facilities finish the printing process, and a new technique in copying systems is also utilized by staff.

The films production staff have the responsibility of writing scripts and filming and editing approximately nine evangelistic, motivational, and training films for reproduction each year. The media productions department develops slide-tape presentations for teaching and promotional purposes. Staff also are involved in the production of television specials, radio spots, and Athletes in Action radio broadcasts.

Each month, members of the tapes department record and distribute 6,000–18,000 tapes, which are used in the movement's discipleship training programs around the world. The focus here is on messages by leading Christian speakers on such topics as management, apologetics, prayer, and Bible study (both method and content). Some specifically evangelistic tapes are also produced here. Finally, media engineering staff contribute to the total effectiveness of the ministry by designing, maintaining, and repairing electronic equipment. They have designed sound equipment for Campus Crusade's musical groups and new types of training devices and slide production equipment.

Whatever we may think of the movement's heavy use of mass media for evangelism and discipleship training, we have to be impressed by this well-conceived, highly sophisticated, and up-to-date operation—its modern technology and the talented staff who are the main reason for its overall effectiveness.

9 Campus Crusade's Ministries Today (II): All Things to All People

> I have begun to believe that the Christian life is a *pilgrimage*, not a *program*; a pilgrimage with people who want to be willing to love, live, and possibly die for Christ, each other, and the world. I have begun to experience what it is like to take the risk of revealing *my* true needs, and to love other Christians enough to let them *help me* when I really hurt—as well as trying to help them.
>
> KEITH MILLER, *The Edge of Adventure*

THE LAY MINISTRY

"The lay ministry is dedicated to serving the local church," Bill Bright explains. "We are committed to the fact that the local pastor and lay people are the key to evangelizing their community, and if properly trained with an understanding of how to share their faith in the power of the Spirit, can be used of God in a revolutionary way, even as the first century Christians."

By the mid-1960s, Campus Crusade's lay ministry was underway in full force. For many years, its major strategy has been focused on lay institutes of evangelism, which include a series of lectures on "such important and basic truths as how to be forgiven and cleansed of sin, how to be filled with the Spirit, how to walk in the Spirit, how to witness in the Spirit, and how to fulfill the Great Commission in this generation." Each of these lectures is followed by an hour-long seminar of a more practical nature, teaching laity how to *do* evangelism. Today the more than 380 lay ministry staff members provide aid to pastors as well as lay people, helping them to establish an ongoing evangelistic and discipleship training strategy for their own churches.

The staff of the lay ministry hope to have mobilized 10,000 churches with movements of evangelism and discipleship by 1982. Each of those churches, then, should have an average of 60–100 committed disciples consistently involved in evangelism, contacting 16,000 people per year, and experiencing church growth from 100 to 400 percent. Two thousand of these churches, moreover, should be mobilized to "adopt" and help train churches overseas. As a servant of the church, this ministry also intends to consult with seminary and denominational leaders in implementing both evangelism and discipleship in their particular areas of influence.

Campus Crusade's lay ministry has been highlighted by Explo '72 and Explo '74, by Vonette Bright's Great Commission Prayer Crusade, by the founding of the Great Commission Training Center in the Philippines (where Asian staff and their disciples confronted some 6.2 million people with the gospel in 1976) and a number of U.S. training centers, and, of course, by the whole Here's Life evangelism and discipleship training strategy.

Although the movement would like to think otherwise, it is only since the Here's Life, America campaign that the lay ministry has really begun to emerge as a significant partner with the institutional church in the United States in discipleship training and evangelism. The major thrust of Here's Life Phase I was carried and financed by local churches working together ecumenically. Phases II and III are concerned specifically with follow-up and discipling, with pastors and lay people winning, building, and sending disciples as the major priority of their ministry.

Out of the Here's Life, Philadelphia campaign has emerged one of Campus Crusade's model discipleship training ministries. It is comprised of a number of local pastors, many of whose churches were involved in Phase I. The Christian Leadership Training Center of Greater Philadelphia meets each Thursday morning for four hours, thirty-three weeks a year, at the Presbyterian Church of the Covenant in Bala Cynwyd, a suburb of Philadelphia. It is led by Carl Combs, director of Here's Life, Philadelphia, and Ron Jenson ("dean" of the center), a local minister of the experimental Church of the Savior in suburban Philadelphia, who specializes in ministry to singles (divorced and never-married people).

Jenson spent a good deal of his seminary education focusing on the concept of discipleship in the local church, researching 175 outstanding "healthy" congregations throughout the United States. He feels strongly that a healthy, vital church is marked by a spirit of "oneness and love that *draws* individuals to Christ." His own experience with Campus Crusade in college demonstrated to him that the movement's small-group discipleship training technique emphasized in its campus ministry needed to be incorporated in the ministry of the local church as well. The issue, in his thinking, is relationships: "I was taught about relationships—at least the fundamental nature of them, even when I was involved with Campus Crusade in 1967–1968. They were already putting a heavy emphasis on small-group dynamics then, in that probably 80 percent of the discipleship training process was relational. Most of it, however, was centered on campus where the ministry has always been focused on small, very loving, intimate fellowships. I think it's only been in recent years that Campus Crusade has really learned how to build *caring* relationships in small groups in the local church. That's where Keith Miller and the 'relational theologians' have been helpful."

Relational theology—developed to a large degree by the Faith at Work movement and spearheaded by Episcopal layman and author Keith Miller, United Presbyterian minister and author Bruce Larson, and Lloyd Ogilvie, senior minister of Hollywood Pres.—teaches that theology is not primarily conceptual (dealing with metaphysical abstractions); it is relational. The task of the theologian and pastor is to help individual Christians relate in an honest and loving way to God, themselves, their neighbors, and the world. Informed by modern psychology and the human potential movement as well as by the Bible and academic theology, this relational emphasis has fostered the coming together of not only church lay people in small groups but also pastors themselves, many of whom, contrary to common belief, are lonely individuals with a poor self-image that inevitably hurts the ministry of their churches.

There are about seventy-five ordained clergy involved with the

Philadelphia Christian Leadership Training Center as of 1978. These men have ranged from storefront pastors of black churches without a high school education to a former fellow of St. Peter's College, Oxford University. They represent fourteen denominations, from independent fundamentalist at one end of the spectrum, to conservative Baptist, to mainline United Presbyterian and United Methodist, to high church Episcopal on the other end (including both charismatics and noncharismatics as well). Regular weekday lectures, with homework, center on a number of principles of church dynamics, with a major focus on church organization, management, and growth; on evangelism and discipling; and on the development of a lifestyle that "radiates love, service, and witness." Guest teachers for this unusual group of clergy (which still does not include women pastors and Catholic priests "because they haven't asked") have ranged from "televangelist" and fundamentalist Baptist preacher Jerry Falwell to black radical evangelical pastor and community organizer John Perkins of Mississippi's Voice of Calvary (the name he gave to the ministry in the beginning).

"When we come together," Jenson says, "we try to make it a very relational time, not just a class. We start by singing and praising the Lord. We pray together and honestly share the successes and failures of our representative ministries almost every week. In our small *agape* groups high church Episcopal priests meet together with fundamentalist Baptist pastors and learn how to love and care for each other. We're very 'up front' about our doctrinal, cultural, and political differences, but we also know that we are filled and controlled by the same Spirit who brings us together and allows us to work effectively together for the Kingdom."

Jenson insists that this small-group emphasis is the key to the success of the Philadelphia Christian Leadership Training Center. Furthermore, it is apparent that the center has strengthened one of the major weaknesses of relational theology as a whole—getting people so much "into themselves" and their own circle that they find it far less important to relate to the world in any meaningful ministry. Campus Crusade believes that real Christian fellowship and unity is possible only in the context of outgoing action encouraged by teaching and training to win, build, and send disciples into the world. Thus the small *agape* groups of this fellowship in Philadelphia are there to motivate pastors to reach out not only to their own church leaders and parishioners but also to the world through spiritual multiplication. This model of ministry will be used by the movement's lay ministry in the establishment of new church-oriented training programs for clergy and laity in this country and throughout the world.

THE INTERNATIONAL STUDENT AND MILITARY MINISTRIES

One of Campus Crusade's smaller and lesser known ministries is its work with internationals studying at colleges, universities, and seminaries in the United States. The international student ministry (ISM) focuses its attention on the 300,000 international students here who will return to their homelands to occupy positions of leadership in the sciences, the arts, and government.

Founded in 1967, this ministry hopes to have 125 qualified and experienced staff in the United States by 1980, with additional staff serving at strategic universities in other countries, and thousands of American volunteers who will demonstrate friendship, love, and concern for these students.

Each ISM staff member centers his or her ministry with internationals around four objectives: First, to develop relationships with international students that ultimately will lead to opportunities for aggressive personal and group evangelism. Second, to disciple internationals. Third, and very important, to influence other Christian movements in this country to reach international students. And finally, to continually develop leadership in the United States and abroad, assuming that reaching and discipling will be an ongoing process.

Although working on some of the same campuses, ISM differs, sometimes significantly, from the campus ministry. Because of the great cultural differences between American collegians and internationals, and among the various racial, ethnic, and national groupings, the movement usually takes on a slower and very patient approach to evangelism, making communication understandable before verbal witness takes place. There is a major emphasis to present the gospel as relevant to students from each particular culture. Supporting this intention, a team of administrative assistants research culturally relevant evangelistic and discipleship training tools and strategies as an ongoing process.

Another lesser known ministry of Campus Crusade for Christ is its military ministry, first established in 1965. The more than 117 staff members provide support for chaplains in all of the services on military bases throughout the country by evangelizing and discipling men and women and their dependents.

The military ministry's staff, associate staff (who have another paying job), and volunteers engage in personal evangelism and follow-up efforts; work closely with denominational chaplains; teach Bible studies; conduct training institutes in military evangelism (TIME), again, developing a culturally relevant strategy for the military; host informal evangelistic breakfasts, luncheons, coffees, teas, and home gatherings; and work with retired armed forces personnel (a good recruiting ground for associate staff).

ATHLETES IN ACTION

Athletes have played an important role in the ministry of Campus Crusade from the beginning. In the early years of the movement at UCLA, all-American football players Don Shinnick, Bob Davenport, and Donn Moomaw (now senior minister of Bel Air Presbyterian Church in Los Angeles) and world decathlon champion Rafer Johnson were active in the work. In 1966, Dave Hannah, a former football standout at Oklahoma State University, who was recruited by the Los Angeles Rams, started what is now known as Athletes in Action (AIA)—with Bill Bright's encouragement—as the sports ministry of the movement. A preseason injury caused Hannah to leave the Rams and engage in his new ministry full-time. "The purpose of this work," he explains, "is to introduce athletes to Christ, then to use the platform they have for evangelism. Now, athletes are no more important to God than anyone else. Yet the world has given them an incredible platform, not just in the U.S., but in other parts of the world as well, where their platform is sometimes even bigger. This visibility is influential, because when spectators and athletes themselves hear the testimonies of our players and see the way they play, it makes an impression. Kids especially are looking for heroes, people to model their lives after. Our players are good. They're coming in first, and that really does influence the kids."

AIA, with a staff of 200, is now the most visible ministry of Campus Crusade, even though many people who watch the teams play are not even aware of the Campus Crusade connection. Hannah put together the first AIA basketball team in 1967; today there are wrestling teams based in Lancaster, Pennsylvania, and Long Beach, California; a gymnastics team in Wheaton, Illinois; a college-level basketball team in Canada; and at AIA headquarters in Tustin, California, the main postcollegiate basketball team plus weight-lifting and track-and-field teams. Soccer is being added as well.

The ministry is already strong in Canada, where, just as in the United States, staff spend considerable time with professional athletes, and full-time staff are moving to Europe and Asia to begin ministries there. During 1976–1977, AIA fielded seven competing teams in all. Wrestling team members John Peterson and Gene Davis achieved international acclaim by winning gold and bronze medals, respectively, at the Montreal Olympics. The U.S. basketball team—the movement's pride and joy—received considerable public attention by soundly defeating two of the top amateur teams in the country, the University of San Francisco and the University of Nevada at Las Vegas. During their 1977–1978 season, moreover, they beat the U.S.S.R. national team by a healthy 94–85. Some 110,000 people attended AIA basketball games in 1976–1977, seeing and hearing the evangelistic half-time presentations, in which players share their faith, with an estimated 20 million spectators viewing the team's four televised games. Stories about AIA have appeared in *Time, Sports Illustrated, The New York Times,* the *Los Angeles Times,* and many other newspapers and magazines. And in 1978 the AIA basketball team competed as the official U.S. team in the World Games in Manila.

AIA players are usually recruited while affiliated with Campus Crusade in college or university, for obvious reasons. Team players, however, are exempted from having to raise their own support. AIA playing seasons are longer and more intense than college seasons, and many of the best known players spend a good deal of time speaking to various groups; consequently, they have little opportunity for personal fund raising. Thus these players are termed associate staff and receive the equivalent salary and benefits their counterparts in other Campus Crusade ministries are paid.

Hannah is very much committed to strengthening the role of women in AIA. "We took a women's basketball team to tour Eastern Europe in 1976–1977, and the women's basketball and volleyball teams will be touring next year too. Women's sports as a whole are in a developmental stage. There's not a great deal of top leadership there yet, and a real battle is taking place in the sports world about women's role and identity. We're just beginning to research this problem from a biblical perspective, and we want to make our contribution here as well."

Dave has high regard for the other major Christian athletes' organization, Fellowship of Christian Athletes (FCA). He notes, however, that AIA uses a different approach from FCA's. "FCA is primarily a *fellowship* of Christian sports men and women. We're a fellowship too, but our fellowship is grounded more in aggressive evangelism and discipleship training. We're activists, so to speak. And the particular strengths of AIA—unlike FCA—are our work with pro athletes, in competing teams, with the media, and internationally. FCA operates only in the U.S., and with a pretty low profile. We respect them very much, and where they're doing our kind of work, we try not to compete."

Blacks are aggressively recruited for AIA teams. About 40–50 percent of the main basketball team are black, among them Irv Kiffin, a particularly effective player in AIA's fast-breaking offense who regularly shares with spectators during half-time his dramatic "rescue" by Christ from five years of heroin addiction.

Basketball is the second biggest spectator sport in the world. In the United States today, Ralph Drollinger is surely one of the most up-

and-coming young basketball players in the sport. A native of San Diego, Drollinger plays center on the AIA team, having played behind Bill Walton at UCLA before going on his own. In 1978, the former UCLA basketball standout turned down a $400,000 no-cut contract with the New Jersey Nets to stay with AIA. (Pro recruiters are now one of Dave Hannah's biggest headaches; they make AIA players increasingly attractive offers.)

Drollinger himself is currently AIA's biggest attraction. "I was heavily involved with Campus Crusade in college at UCLA," he declares. "One of the AIA staff members discipled me during my freshman year. By the end of my senior year, joining AIA just seemed the logical thing to do. As a high schooler, I was already motivated toward pro basketball. I wanted to be a millionaire, and the pros looked like the way to do it. But when, as a new Christian at UCLA, I studied the Scriptures, it became clear to me that money should not be my motive in playing basketball. Rather, I should invest my life for eternity, not just for retirement."

Ralph admits that, although there are exceptions, most players at AIA don't intend, and are not expected, to stay with the ministry more than a few years. He himself has made a commitment through 1979–1980, after which seminary seems like a real possibility (he'd like to become an evangelist), though the pros are still not completely out of his thinking. "The money thing is something I continue to struggle with from time to time, because I'm only human," Drollinger explains. "But God has really protected my desires in this area. I don't want to be wealthy and flaunt it. I am very much contented with my present minimal salary, of which I'm able to save 50 percent and give 20 percent away. My living environment is great, and all my needs are met."

The fact is that AIA players play for God. "The difference between us and many of those we play is that we're doing it for someone other than ourselves," Drollinger concludes. "This is demonstrated by the way we play. We have some of the best teamwork I've seen or can imagine, because we're not playing from *selfish* motivation—personal gain, worldly adulation, and money. As players for God's work, we really try to love each other, our opponents, and the spectators as well. When people complain that we're all just plastic smiles and are always trying to shove the Four Spiritual Laws down other people, they simply don't know and understand us. We feel that this is the best way to get the gospel across, and we're convinced that a personal relationship with God is the most important thing in the world. What better way, then, can we love someone else than by sharing that relationship in a loving and affirming manner?"

Anyone who has seen AIA teams in action know that Drollinger is telling the truth. The fact that they are good and getting better has attracted media and public attention. But that all-important difference—unselfish teamwork—is what really affects sports enthusiasts when they see a game. It is AIA's way of demonstrating the gospel as well as proclaiming it.

THE CHRISTIAN EMBASSY

Without a doubt, the Christian Embassy in Washington, D.C., has been the most controversial ministry associated with Campus Crusade for Christ. Several years ago, Bill Bright was addressing one of the movement's executive seminars. He was concerned about the spiritual life of government leaders in the nation's capital, and, almost parenthetically, remarked that Washington needed a Christian Embassy, a base for aggressive evangelism among those government leaders and others in the city. Rolfe McCollister, a wealthy businessman and a senior partner in a Baton Rouge law firm, took Bill up on the idea. Both of them got together several other men interested in the project and began looking for property. It was their feeling that to minister effectively to government leaders and the diplomatic community, an elegant embassylike house in a fashionable neighborhood was needed. Bill knew about and respected other Christian movements in Washington—the prayer breakfasts and Fellowship House with Harold Hughes, Mark Hatfield, and, later, Charles Colson—but, in his thinking, none of them was engaged in aggressive evangelism and discipleship, Campus Crusade's primary methodology.

In 1975, Bright asked his former personal assistant, then directing the Campus Crusade ministry in Latin America, to become director of the Christian Embassy. Rodney "Swede" Anderson is a graduate of the University of Colorado and Dallas Theological Seminary and had been student body president of both schools. It was extremely difficult for Swede to accept the position. He comments, "My wife and I had developed a vital relationship with our Latin American colleagues—Colombian, Argentinian, Guatemalan, and Mexican— one in which we were so close, both in our work and friendship, that I really didn't want to leave. But we prayed about it together, and my colleagues then encouraged me to accept the post. We began work at the embassy in February 1976."

Anderson likens the style of the Christian Embassy's ministry to that of the movement's campus ministry. The building itself, with its gracious atmosphere, has been used primarily for evangelistic gatherings—luncheons, teas, and dinners—with a featured speaker (Bill and Vonette spend a few days in Washington each month), testimonies, and an invitation for those present to receive Christ after the meeting. "But the bulk of our ministry takes place all around the city," Swede explains, "because, just as in our campus ministry, we go to people where they are and minister to them there. So, one day I might be involved in a Bible study at the Pentagon, the next day, somewhere else. Each week I have a Bible study with several members of Congress. Then there are the ever-present breakfast, luncheon, and dinner appointments throughout the city. Most of our staff here follow the same model of ministry, going where the people are."

Anderson insists that, from the start, Bill assured him that the Christian Embassy would not take on a political character—right, left or center. "I asked Bill whether the particular political convictions of staff members would be a factor in their selection. He said absolutely not. We've been called here to lead men and women to Christ and help them grow in their faith and share it with others. If, for one minute, I thought that Bill intended otherwise, I would have never become involved. And I think I can say the same for most of our staff. In terms of my own experience with Campus Crusade in

Latin America, I was deeply touched and changed, really, by the faith of our brothers and sisters who live in poverty there, who—without hesitation—take their faith and all it requires into the marketplace, to change the society in which they live. The last thing I'd want to be involved in is any evangelistic strategy that links evangelism with right-wing politics."

Swede's reference here is to an accusation made by *Sojourners*, a radical evangelical magazine published in Washington, that Bill Bright and the Christian Embassy were linked together with a group of wealthy right-wing businessmen and conservative politicians to elect Christians of a very conservative political stripe to national office in the general election of 1976. (More will be said about this charge in Chapter 12.)

The Christian Embassy mansion was sold, finally, in the summer of 1978, just two years after its dedication, largely because of zoning problems. But the ministry remains, and its purpose and character are not likely to change.

10 Campus Crusade's Ministries Today (III): Raising Up the Oppressed

The Spirit of the Lord is upon me,
Because he anointed me to preach good tidings to the poor:
He hath sent me to proclaim release to the captives,
And recovering of sight to the blind,
To set at liberty them that are bruised,
To proclaim the acceptable year of the Lord.
LUKE 4:18, 19 (Phillips)

Some of Campus Crusade's ministries are specifically geared to the social dimension of the gospel. They work with people who have suffered social abuses—racial discrimination, poverty, political injustice, and the like. But, in the context of fighting these abuses, the movement's social ministries still center their focus on winning, building, and sending—on evangelism and discipleship training.

P.S. MINISTRIES

P.S. ministries is an outreach of Campus Crusade in penal institutions. *P.S.* stands for *personal Savior*, "the only solution to the penal situation." It also means *prodigal sons*, because the Christian message is for everyone, and who cannot say, "There but for the grace of God go I?" P.S. stands for *personal solution* as well, because Christ came to deal with individuals. It means *penal solution*, because changed lives will contribute to a changed society. And finally, P.S. , stands for *programmed solutions*, which are presented through films, correspondence courses, Bible study, and group and personal counseling.

The goals of P.S. ministries are to make the gospel available to each inmate in North America, to disciple those who respond to the message, and to organize social-spiritual fellowships on the outside ("network" activities) to assist parolees and probationers and their families to find Christian answers to their problems within society.

"In the U.S. we have somewhere in the neighborhood of 250,000 people incarcerated at any given time in prison," explains P.S. ministries director Larry Benton. "I think you could double or even triple that number if you also take into account all the jails. Then multiply the figure by three if you include the probationers and parolees. So we're really talking about a couple of million Americans. Furthermore, if we recognize that each of these individuals affects the lives of at least three to five others, we can discern a large "penal subculture" of individuals who feel put down, alienated, and rejected both by our society as a whole and by Christianity. P.S., therefore, works not only in penal institutions themselves, but also on the street and in our neighborhoods. We seek to follow-up these people after they're released, trying to be a bridge for them to re-enter society and become a part of the church."

Benton feels strongly that "Christians should be active in their communities ministering to all 'disenfranchised' people, those incarcerated and those—both in and outside prison—who are suffering social abuses. If we had more sensitivity at that level, we'd have far less crime. Basically, as believers, we have no right to turn our backs on the unlovely—people who aren't like ourselves and who often have a poor self-image because they are 'different.' Remember, when one Christian ignores the oppressed and disenfranchised, the church as a whole gets blamed. Furthermore, Christians need to proclaim *and* demonstrate forgiveness, a forgiveness that also forgets. The church simply cannot be 'successful' if it doesn't practice forgiveness."

Larry knows what he's talking about first-hand. On the morning of April 7, 1970, while he was away from home, a man forced his way into the Benton household, assaulted Larry's wife Beverly and left her tied up, ransacking the house and stealing the family car. When the intruder was finally caught and put in jail, Larry and Beverly Benton felt compelled to contact him and express their forgiveness. This led to a regular correspondence with him and a number of personal visits during the next several years he was incarcerated. The incident, Larry and Beverly found out, was preceded by thirty-five years behind bars for the intruder. Larry was finally able to get the man paroled—he'd become a Christian while in Folsom Prison—and he spent one good year on the outside before he was jailed again for eighteen months. The Bentons kept up their contact with him. Things changed, moreover, when he was released again. Now, according to the P.S. ministries director, "he's doing very well, has a job, and is steady as a rock." This experience, then, opened Beverly's and Larry's eyes to the need for a Campus Crusade prison ministry.

Incidentally, Larry was also instrumental in securing former Black Panther Eldridge Cleaver's initial release from jail upon his return to the United States from France, where he'd already been converted. Both Beverly and Larry spent a couple of afternoons with Cleaver and his wife at the Alameda County Jail in Oakland. Larry's report then quickly got into the hands of Art De Moss, a wealthy Campus Crusade board member, who visited Eldridge and put up half the required bail money. After his release, Cleaver insisted on he and his wife, Kathleen, being baptized in the pool at Arrowhead Springs, despite the movement's general policy of not allowing sacramental rites to be performed within its ministry.

Prior to establishing P.S. ministries in 1974, Benton had been manager of the Arrowhead Springs Hotel before his conversion. Thereafter, the graduate of the University of California, Berkeley focused on the movement's international ministries, and helped to start the *Agape* movement.

A number of different kinds of staff are recruited for P.S. work. Para-chaplains are full-time staff members, trained by P.S. in a manner similar to that of the *Agape* movement. Their ministry team assignments are to statewide supervisory duties or to specific institutions where they serve two-year terms as assistants to institutional chaplains, just as in the military ministry. Associate chaplains are associate staff who receive the same training as para-chaplains, but they are usually assigned to smaller institutions or to network supervision and operations more generally. Volunteer chaplains are associate staff who have not had P.S. intensive training. Their ministry team assignments focus on city and county jails and network outreach. Volunteers are simply trained lay men and women who visit penal institutions at least weekly and help develop community network ministries.

New staff members are trained for P.S. ministries in ministry development, institutional orientation, cross-cultural communication, biblical principles for daily living, management techniques, and personal counseling. In most cases, this is done through a programmed training structure involving an Institute of Biblical Studies (four weeks), new staff training (two weeks), financial support development (six weeks, during which new staff raise their own support), P.S. intensive training (three months), and continuing on-the-job training (two years). At present, P.S. has only about thirty staff members, but it hopes to recruit significantly larger numbers in the future.

INTERNATIONAL MINISTRIES

Campus Crusade's international ministries have grown consistently since the mid-1960s. Although each has sought to implement the movement's strategies developed in the United States, the focus has increasingly been on winning, building, and sending men and women into their own particular culture. And, although in many cases the first staff members serving in Latin America and overseas were Americans, there has been a major attempt within the movement to recruit staff leadership from the indigenous populations of each of the more than ninety-seven countries of Campus Crusade's international ministries. Indeed, the movement's cross-cultural evangelism and discipleship training in some nations is very different from that employed in the United States. Latin American and overseas staff simply do not fit U.S. stereotypes, good or bad. There are currently over 1,925 indigenous staff working outside the United

States in addition to more than 215 international representatives from America based in those countries.

The Asian ministry, with headquarters in Quezon City, the Philippines, has 440 staff members and is directed by American, Bailey Marks. In 1976, Here's Life was begun in the Indian state of Kerala, and 44,000 workers were mobilized and trained for the saturation of the state's 22 million people. The movement's workers traveled the crowded cities and mountainous tea plantations, going from house to house to share the gospel. Large evangelistic meetings were also held in the evenings. According to official estimates, Here's Life, Kerala, resulted in nearly 1.5 million people receiving Christ through person-to-person contacts, and 390,000 more in the evangelistic gatherings. By 1977, Here's Life had also been initiated in the Philippines, Taiwan, Hong Kong, Malaysia, and Singapore, in a manner culturally suitable for each country involved.

Another American, Don Myers, directs the movement's African ministry from Nairobi, Kenya, assisted by a staff of 180. During 1976–1977, Campus Crusade staff members in Africa completed an audio-training unit, enabling them to provide essential discipleship training to millions of Christians who cannot read (70 percent of Africa's total population). Utilizing dramatized dialogue lessons written and recorded by Africans themselves, the unit hopes to train Africa's illiterates in the basics of Christian discipleship even before they learn to read.

Kundan Massey, a Pakistani, directs the movement's small Middle East ministry from Tehran, Iran. His staff of fifty feel that, for witness for Christ to be effective in a predominantly Muslim culture, there will have to be a great deal of miracle-seeking prayer and new evangelistic and training techniques developed among all Christians living in the Mideast. Thus at the present time, the Great Commission Prayer Crusade is a dominant part of the ministry.

The movement's Canadian ministry (based in British Columbia and closely linked to U.S. operations) is directed by Marvin Kehler, who oversees the work of 120 staff members. Following the Here's Life, Edmonton, Alberta, campaign of 1976, a large-scale mission conference—"World Thrust"—was held in that city. Sponsored by

Campus Crusade's *Agape* movement, the conference utilized multimedia presentations, special speakers, singing groups, and personnel from various Christian organizations to challenge people with a vision of helping to reach the world for Christ. Of the 2,000 individuals who attended, 259 made commitments to take the gospel overseas sometime in the future.

The same kind of structural chain of command used by Campus Crusade in the United States is followed, by and large, in the movement's international ministries. Each of the continental ministries (Asia, Africa, Middle East, Europe, and Latin America) is headed by a director who reports to Bill Bright himself (assisted here by Frank Obien, his special assistant for international affairs) and oversees the work of all the national ministry directors in his jurisdiction. National directors, of course, oversee the ministries of Campus Crusade in their particular countries and all their staff.

Kalevi Lehtinen, a priest of the (Lutheran) Church of Finland, directs the European ministry from Mülheim, Germany, and oversees the work of 310 staff members. Typical of the Finns in his home town of Helsinki and 95 percent of all Finns, Lehtinen belonged to the state church from childhood. But he had no personal relationship with God until high school, where, he remembers, there were "more important things in life, like athletics, girls, and student government, at least in the beginning. But as a member of his school's student government, he felt responsible to help organize a Christian conference. During this conference, the "peace and joy I saw in those Christians" compelled him to receive Christ personally and, at the age of seventeen, commit his life to full-time Christian service. Lehtinen received a master's degree in theology from the University of Helsinki in 1963 and was ordained in 1964.

Upon graduation from university, Lehtinen became an evangelist and pastor and a teacher. Then, in 1966, he was invited to be one of eight Finnish delegates to the Billy Graham–sponsored World Congress on Evangelism in Berlin. Bill Bright, one of the major speakers at the congress, impressed Lehtinen and his wife Eine, with his message, and it wasn't long before both of them joined staff. In 1967, Kalevi began the movement's European ministry as director of the work in Finland. Soon afterward, the University Ambassadors (about seventy of them) arrived in Europe from Campus Crusade in the United States to help expand the ministry throughout the continent. Now the European ministry has a staff, three-quarters of whom are European. In January 1977, Kalevi and Eine Lehtinen together were dedicated as the new director of affairs for Europe. By and large, they work and travel together as a ministry team, a major reason both of them joined staff in the first place. "I would say that in Scandinavia," Lehtinen relates, "we have not had women's liberation as a movement, because women have been free for centuries. If I am not mistaken, Finland was the first or second country in the world to give women the right to vote. Women have been accepted as equal to men in Scandinavia because they are human beings. I believe that women have the same intrinsic value and are just as intelligent as men. Thus, if God gives spiritual gifts to women—as he does— calling them to ministry, we have the responsibility of creating structures of ministry where those gifts can be worked out. Women are very active in the ministry of Campus Crusade in Europe, and we have had women directors of campus ministry in the past, in Finland and Sweden, at least. Women's liberation is simply not the divisive issue in Scandinavia and other European countries that it is in the U.S."

The work of the movement in Europe is 70–80 percent concentrated on the university campus, and the strongest national ministries are in Finland, England (with over seventy staff members), Germany, Holland, and Switzerland—all with heavily Protestant populations. But the ministry in the Irish Republic, predominantly Catholic, is growing. The work of Campus Crusade there is taking place increasingly with Catholic laity and priests; even the archbishop is friendly to the movement. (For cultural reasons, the Irish staff refused to launch Here's Life in their country.) Europe is one of the most popular of all Campus Crusade fields and has one of the lowest turnovers of staff.

"Europe is often regarded by American Christians as more 'culturally liberal' than the U.S.," Lehtinen declares. "Clearly, among European Christians—most of them, anyway—activities like drinking, smoking, and dancing simply aren't an issue, since they are an integral part of our way of life. And we don't make an issue of these

things in Campus Crusade either. Likewise, however, many European Christians look at the U.S. as more culturally liberal than Europe
because of its affluent lifestyles. So it's largely a matter of interpretation—who's culturally liberal and who's conservative. Most human
values are relative. They are products of our family life, education,
and traditions, and they have all too easily become questions of right
and wrong in a spiritual sense—needlessly. For instance, in Europe
there are Campus Crusade staff members from fascist backgrounds
and others who are socialists, and it doesn't hurt our working
relationships at all. We emphasize that if a person is controlled by the
Holy Spirit, the Spirit will help that person make the right decisions
in all practical situations."

Sergio Garcia Romo, a Mexican national, directs Campus Crusade's Latin American ministry, based in Cuernavaca, Mexico. He
oversees a staff of over 450 full-time workers, most of whom are
Latin Americans, and more than 700 volunteers. As in Europe, the
ministry's emphasis has been mainly on college and university
students—on campus ministry. But gradually that work has expanded to include pastors and lay people, growing number of whom,
especially in Colombia, are Catholic priests and laity.

Garcia was converted at the age of seventeen and joined Campus
Crusade staff in 1961 after a teaching career in law, having been
very much impressed by Bill Bright's theology of the Spirit-filled
life. In 1962, Garcia started the movement's Latin American ministry in Mexico City, where he directed the Mexican ministry until
January 1977. At this point, Garcia became director of the whole
ministry in Central and South America, succeeding an Anglo U.S.
citizen, Swede Anderson, who is currently back in the States. The
movement now is established in every Latin American nation,
where, because of the predominant poverty, staff are allowed to take
up to four years to raise their support while they are paid by Campus
Crusade out of its own funds (as opposed to six weeks given to most
new U.S. staff).

"I believe that in Latin America there is today a state of great
spiritual hunger," Garcia explains. "And this hunger is centered in
the masses of poor people who are living in the midst of revolutionary social and political change. The population is growing dramati-

cally. People are moving to the cities at an ever-increasing rate (Mexico City will be the largest city in the world by A.D. 2000), and the political situation in any given country can change completely almost overnight. You can breathe and touch revolution here." This is one reason, Garcia feels, that the Here's Life follow-up and discipling strategy has worked better in Latin America than elsewhere in the world.

Garcia goes on to say, "We want our staff to adopt a radical style in their ministries. Not in a political sense, but in a manner that accurately reflects the true meaning of the word *radical*, getting to the bottom of the issues. [*Radical* comes from the Latin *rādix*, root, or that which lies at the foundation.] We believe that true *agape* lies behind the Christian message. God *loves* you. . . . Therefore, we are trying to build the *agape* person here, one whose life of faith will be marked indisputably by that quality. All new staff and student leaders embark on a mission to the rural villages for three weeks during their training (many of our staff come to us from relatively well-to-do urban backgrounds). We send them out for three weeks with just a toothbrush and three to six dollars equivalent for bus fares, not even with a change of clothes. They go out into the countryside two by two to proclaim and demonstrate the gospel of the Kingdom. These university-educated men and women offer their services to the villagers for food and shelter, working in the villages and in the fields. They identify completely with the rural farmers, and at night they ask permission to share from the Scriptures. I've done it myself. I left my credit cards at home, dressed like the typical rural farmer, and made my way into the villages for three weeks. We call ourselves 'heavenly beggars,' because, in fact—in the words of D. T. Niles—Christians are best described as 'beggars telling other beggars where to find bread.'"

AGAPE

Agape (noun) and *agapao* (verb) are Greek words used in the New Testament to describe God's self-giving, unconditional love. They are also used there to convey the spirit God wants his people to demonstrate to each other and all men and women. *Agape*, furthermore, expresses the essential nature of God and can only be known from the action it prompts: Love is something you *do*. Christian love is the fruit of the Holy Spirit. And self-will is the negation of the love of God that seeks the welfare of all, works no ill to anybody, and seeks actively the opportunity to do good to all people.

Initiated in February 1973, the *Agape* movement is Campus Crusade's most social concern–oriented ministry. Modeled after the Peace Corps, it seeks to place staff primarily in Third World developing countries, to help in their social and economic development. Teams already established include construction and maintenance personnel, secretaries, doctors, dentists, nurses, lab technicians, agricultural experts, engineers of all types, administrators, and teachers in all subject areas.

The specific goals of the *Agape* movement are four: (1) to help meet the physical needs of communities and nations; (2) to make a clear and simple presentation of the message of Jesus Christ to people of all nations; (3) to train and disciple Christian nationals to reach their own people with the claims of Christ; and (4) to aid and cooperate with existing missionary movements to help fulfill these goals. Approximately 50 percent of the staff's time is devoted to ministry needs.

Staff training includes ministry development, vocational orientation, language instruction, area studies, team relationship building, personal behavioral instruction, cross-cultural communications, biblical studies, preventive health care, and management training. *Agape* movement staff receive seven months of intensive training, including four months' cross-cultural training in South Central Los Angeles and Watts. As a rule, teams of approximately four to ten people of similar or related vocational backgrounds are formed and sent out under a team leader to practice their vocations and to train nationals in their skills in one area.

The *Agape* movement currently has only about 110 staff members working overseas, in addition to a number of office personnel and trainers, two-thirds of whom are under 30, based in the United States. The first movement candidates were assigned to their two-year terms in the field in February 1974, and, at the end of eighteen

months, agricultural, educational, administrative, and medical teams
were serving on four continents. A high percentage of current staff
members—perhaps 60 percent—in training and in the field are
women. At his point, countries receiving *Agape* movement staff
include Liberia, Swaziland, Hong Kong, Korea, the Philippines,
Germany, Austria, and the United States; some twenty-five nations
have requested 3,000 additional staff to fill positions in their lands.
And Bill Bright hopes to have recruited and sent into the field the
incredible number of 100,000 Agape movement staff in the next few
years.

Directed by Larry Poland, a behavioral scientist with a Ph.D. from
Purdue University, the *Agape* movement has a special interest in the
healing arts. "One of the things that motivated Bill to start the
movement," Poland explains, "is his great interest in *paramedics*
who can treat perhaps 75 percent of all patients who walk into a
M.D.'s office. He feels that a substantial number of the world's sick
can be successfully treated by thousands of paramedics in our
movement—people who can be trained inexpensively over a relatively short period of time."

Poland goes on to say that "the world mission is changing
dramatically. The traditional missionary concept is dying quickly
and may never emerge again. Many countries simply don't want
foreign nationals working as full-time proselytizers for an alien faith.
They want technical assistance; and we can get our people trained in
agriculture, technology, and medicine into a nation where traditional
missionaries have been outlawed for years. We can do this mainly
because of their skills in these areas, but also because we can promise
the government of the nations we seek to serve that our staff will (1)
meet their required standards of education and training; (2) have the
highest standard of morality (a very important attribute today,
especially in socialist countries where strict moral standards are often
enforced); (3) not be dependent on your money; (4) not become
involved in politics; and (5) keep any money they receive for services
in your country. Thus, we have no problem getting our people in.
We just need many more staff members to meet the thousands of
requests for our personnel. In Luke 4:16–21, Jesus indicates very

clearly that his message isn't simply spiritual. It is physical, mental, emotional, and social as well. Christians have got to understand this."

Larry is part of Campus Crusade's ministry because "Bill made me feel from the beginning that I'm bigger than an organization. I'm part of a movement that wants to help change the world, and I feel that I'm doing just that personally and with like-minded people. I experience an incredible amount of fellowship and joy with my colleagues. And I've never worked with a more highly motivated, competent, and visionary staff in my life."

THE INTERCULTURAL MINISTRY

From the movement's beginnings at UCLA in 1951, racial and ethnic minorities have been represented among students, staff, and lay workers (Rafer Johnson was the first black to gain visibility within its ranks in the 1950s). In 1974, Campus Crusade's intercultural ministry (ICM) was established. The United States is a composite of colors and creeds. More than 50 million people in the United States—blacks, Mexican-Americans, Asian-Americans, Native Americans, and others—fit into the category of ethnic and racial minorities. And these individuals are most often oppressed by and alienated from the mainstream of American life socially, economically, and politically. Embittered by this alienation, they often reject Christianity as a tool of "Western imperialism," thinking that Christianity and Western culture are synonymous. ICM was organized to repudiate that notion by taking the gospel into specific racial and ethnic communities in a way that would be affirming of and relevant to their cultures. The ministry has consisted of staff representing the four major minority groups in the United States working together, and separately when necessary, to evangelize and disciple these communities. Unfortunately, ICM has not yet been able to "get it together" structurally. Different ethnic and racial groups have different problems, and staff recruitment has been difficult. ICM still exists, but it is in transition.

The movement's black student ministry, however, is currently being strengthened. Although blacks are sought by all of Campus

Crusade's ministries, the black student ministry is now the most visible. Its purpose is to build campus movements of black Christian leaders. These movements already have been established at black colleges, such as Morehouse, Morris Brown, Spelman, Clark, Miles, Lawson State, Langston, Grambling, and Jackson State. There are also black Campus Crusade student ministries at major state universities, such as Michigan, Kansas, Illinois, and Arizona. To help solve the problem of black staff recruitment, Campus Crusade has adopted a policy of allowing blacks in the United States several years if necessary to raise their own support rather than the usual six weeks. During that time, black staff are paid by the movement directly because, for many reasons, raising one's financial support in the black community is difficult.

Closely associated with, but not part of, Campus Crusade's black ministries is the *Harambe* movement, with headquarters in the First Baptist Church of North Fontana, California. *Harambe* derives from a Swahili word meaning come together. Born in 1974, it has specialized in organizing annual evangelistic gatherings in black communities across the country, featuring such speakers as black evangelist Tom Skinner, social activist Jesse Jackson, and famed gospel musicians James Cleveland and André Crouch. Chuck Singleton, pastor of North Fontana Baptist and a Campus Crusade associate staff member, uses the organization's materials and basic strategies, but there are no full-time workers, just a good number of volunteers in numerous American cities. The major emphasis of *Harambe*, moreover, is reaching black men and women on the street, not just on the college campus or in the church. The movement wants to train blacks to go into their communities to tell others, black youths especially, about Christ.

E.V. Hill is one of the most influential black clergy in Southern California and, for that matter, in the entire country. Senior minister of the large Mt. Zion Baptist Church in South Central Los Angeles, he has worked closely with Campus Crusade. Several years ago, Hill, a strong integrationist as opposed to a separatist, established his World Christian Training Center (WCTC) to train Christians in the Watts area to share their faith in their own neighborhoods on a block-by-block basis, starting Bible studies and talking to their neighbors about Christ. Since its inception, training center work has spread to the black communities of Houston, Detroit, Philadelphia, and a number of other cities in the United States.

As the ministry of WCTC grew, E.V. Hill began to recruit more men and women to implement his block-by-block evangelism strategy. Roy Rosedale, coordinator of ministry training for the Agape movement and a pacifist Mennonite, responded by working out an arrangement with WCTC to send in-training *Agape* staff to South Central Los Angeles on weekends to work on the project while they stayed with a black family and attended a black church. The program was so successful that almost all *Agape* movement and international ministries staff candidates spend nearly four full months of intensive cross-cultural training there. Both Mt. Zion Baptist Church and WCTC have integrated ministries.

Willie Richardson, black pastor of Stronghold Baptist Church in West Philadelphia, has been an avid supporter of Here's Life, Philadelphia, and works closely with Campus Crusade in general. Although very affirmative of Bill Bright and the movement as a whole, Richardson hopes that Campus Crusade will take further positive steps to develop a strong ministry to and with blacks in the United States. "The movement has been seen by black pastors, especially, as having too much of a white emphasis in its work, and a definite lack of positive recognition of black churches without *paternalism*. Whites can learn just as much from black churches as vice versa. In 1977 there were only ten full-time black staff members of Campus Crusade. Blacks have never separated evangelism from social concern the way whites have, and this is simply not the way blacks want to develop their ministries—to think of those two aspects of the gospel as mutually exclusive. At the present time, moreover, Campus Crusade has been limited in its outreach because it tends very much to *stress* verbal witnessing, while making social concern a matter of *secondary* importance. But we remain confident of Bill Bright's genuine interest in our people, and we have been assured that black ministry in the movement will be strengthened."

Bill does have a strong interest in building up Campus Crusade's black ministries and has taken steps to implement a new strategy of black-directed evangelism and discipleship training. "It's only been since Martin Luther King, Jr., that large numbers of Americans, Christians among them, have been motivated to *do* anything about the race problem in the U.S.," he admits. "I didn't know King personally, but I think God used him to help right a terrible injustice in our society."

PART V

VISION

11 Bill Bright the Pragmatist, Bill Bright the Visionary

There is nothing which is quite so much needed throughout the world-wide mission of the Christian religion as a fresh summons to the impossible. For is this not precisely what Christ gave when He launched His world-wide program? Can those of us who are called upon to lead forward His world mission do less? . . . It is urgently desirable that we come to see and then afford fresh demonstrations of the fact that in the sublime enterprise of making Christ known, loved, obeyed, and exemplified in life and human relationships it is easier to accomplish very great, bafflingly difficult, even impossible things than the easy, the simple, and the possible.

JOHN R. MOTT, *The Present-Day Summons*

FULFILLING THE GREAT COMMISSION IN OUR GENERATION

Born in 1865 in New York, John R. Mott, "world citizen," was one of the greatest Christian leaders of his time. A graduate of Cornell University and a Methodist layman, he was one of the Mt. Hermon Hundred, the group of students attending the conference convened by the Student Y.M.C.A. and Dwight L. Moody in Mt. Hermon, Massachusetts, in July 1886, who signed a pledge declaring, "We are willing and desirous, if God permits, to become foreign missionaries." Out of this pivotal conference emerged the Student Volunteer Movement for Foreign Missions (SVM), of which Mott was chairman of the executive committee from 1888 to 1920. The delegates at Mt. Hermon carried their enthusiasm back to their campuses. By the end of 1887, the number of student volunteers for foreign mission service had grown to over 2,000, and in 1888, the SVM was established officially. Later, at Mott's instigation, the movement adopted its famous "watchword"—the evangelization of the world in this generation. For the next three decades, this organization was to enlist the very ablest men and women on the college and university campuses of the United States and send them to the far corners of the earth. Between 1886 and 1936 it enrolled just under 50,000 student volunteers, more than 13,000 of whom sailed to foreign mission fields—a figure constituting about half of the total number of missionaries actually sent out during that time.

Gradually, John R. Mott became the world's foremost leader of student-motivated evangelism. From 1888 to 1915, he was also national secretary of the Student Y.M.C.A. Then, in 1895, Mott helped organize the World's Student Christian Federation (WSCF), an organization now based in Geneva, to unite Christian student movements in all lands.

By the end of his lifetime, John R. Mott had been chairman of the International Missionary Council (now part of the World Council of Churches); had been offered (but turned down) the ambassadorship to China by Woodrow Wilson, the general secretaryship of the Federal Council of Churches (now National Council of Churches), the deanship of Yale Divinity School, and a professorship of biblical studies at Stanford University; and had been approached with reference to the presidencies of Oberlin College and of Princeton University.

Despite his unflinching theological conservatism—Methodist pietism, not fundamentalism—and his passionate desire to evangelize the world for Christ in his generation, Mott traveled mainly in ecumenical circles, lectured and recruited at the world's best universities, and became friends with world political leaders everywhere. Mott was respected equally by church leaders and government officials wherever he went. He was one of the first editorial board members of *Christianity and Crisis*, the magazine founded in the early 1940s by Reinhold Niebuhr and John C. Bennett, eminent social ethics professors at Union Theological Seminary in New York City, in opposition to the stated pacifism of *The Christian Century* in World War II.

One of the most controversial aspects of John R. Mott's life, ironically, was his constant use of the SVM's watchword. The task of evangelizing the world in Mott's generation, of course, seemed impossible to most Christians of his time. Nevertheless, despite the fact that generations have passed since the watchword was adopted, and the world remains unevangelized, Mott would not be discouraged even if he were alive today. He felt strongly that the ideal was and is realizable if individual Christians everywhere make it the governing principle of their lives. It simply emphasizes, he argued, the urgency of the world's evangelization, that it is a task for living men and women on behalf of men and women now living.

More than thirty years after the adoption of the watchword by the SVM, John R. Mott addressed its 1924 convention in Indianapolis, explaining to those in attendance how the priority of the watchword had affected his own life:

> I can truthfully say that next to the decision to take Christ as the leader and Lord of my life, the watchword has had more influence than all other ideals and objectives combined to widen my horizon and enlarge my conception of the Kingdom of God; to hold me steadfast in the face of criticism, opposition, and other obstacles to the great Christ-commanded purpose of seeking first the Kingdom of God; to stimulate my personal preparation for service to my generation; to deepen my conviction as to the necessity of furthering the more intensive aspects of the missionary enterprise such as educational missions, the building up of strong native churches, and the raising up of an able indigenous leadership; to recognize and promote the essential strategy involved in establishing an adequate home base, and in Christianizing the impact of the so-called Christian nations on the non-Christian world; to appreciate vividly both the social and the individual aspects of the Christian gospel and likewise their essential unity; to see the necessity of linking together the Christian students of all lands and races, and of raising up from among them an army of well-furnished, God-called, heroic Volunteers; to realize and live under the spell of the great urgency of the task of giving each generation an adequate opportunity to know Christ; and, above all, to deepen acquaintance with God and to throw us back on him for ever fresh accessions of superhuman wisdom, love, and power.

It was the activity of Mott's student volunteers and their successors—idealistic and truly ecumenical—in the mission fields of the world that laid the foundation for the contemporary ecumenical movement as a whole.

At the beginning of his ministry, Bill Bright made the "fulfillment of the Great Commission in our generation" the watchword and single goal of Campus Crusade, taking up where Mott left off, so to speak. "Go therefore and make disciples of all nations, baptizing them in the name of the Father and the Son and the Holy Spirit, teaching them to observe all that I commanded you; and lo, I am with you always, even to the end of the age" (Matthew 28:19,20 NASB). For Bill, "True discipling of Christians involves evangelism and true evangelism involves discipling of believers." Helping to fulfill the Great Commission in toto is not simply a matter of evangelism per se but of building and sending disciples as well.

Bright has set 1980 as the target date for the "initial fulfillment" of the Great Commission, even in communist lands. He says, "We may set forth a definition of the initial fulfillment of the Great Commission. It is the preaching of the gospel to such an extent that the percentage of those who are *known* to have heard it will be sufficiently great as to suggest that the rest of the world has also heard the message, either from primary or secondary sources. This does not mean that by 1980 every country will be 'Christianized' or even that a majority will become Christians, but it does mean that everyone who has the ability to comprehend will have a chance to hear the gospel. Again, I must emphasize that the widespread proclamation of the gospel is only the beginning; we must not stop there. We must go on with the objective of giving every person possible an opportunity to receive Christ personally, and then seek to include them in the local, visible body of believers, the church, where they will be taught and encouraged to grow in maturity in their Christian lives."

At the conclusion of Campus Crusade's statement of faith, signed by all staff members, the issue is made clear: "The Lord Jesus Christ commanded all believers to proclaim the gospel throughout the world and to disciple men and women of every nation. The fulfillment of the Great Commission requires that all worldly and personal ambitions be subordinated to a total commitment to 'him who loved us and gave himself for us.'... I hereby... pledge myself to help fulfill the Great Commission in our generation, depending on the Holy Spirit to guide and empower me."

THE LAST THINGS

If there is any greatness in Bill Bright, it has very little to do with his personality, his looks, his intelligence, or even his pragmatism. It is centered, rather, on his vision and on his rare ability to instill that vision in his staff and supporters, to make them want to do what he wants them to do. Vision suggests imaginative foresight, the conviction that there is more to life than we now experience, a grasp of the possibility of the impossible. Vision and a belief in progress are closely related, and Bill's vision is a result of his eschatology, his theology of the Last Things.

Because of the nondoctrinal character of Campus Crusade and the wide diversity of opinion within the organization itself and within Christianity generally, Bill rarely talks about eschatology as such. Most modern-day evangelicals probably are premillennialists. Christ will come again literally, physically, and imminently to establish his 1000-year reign of righteousness and peace on earth (Revelation 20). However, premillennial theology for the most part (dispensationalism especially) has put a damper on Christian social concern and reform because of the imminency of Christ's return and the immediacy (relatively speaking) of the consummation of the Kingdom of God and its perfect society. Thus premillennial revivalists of the twentieth century, including Billy Graham, have focused almost all their attention on getting people "saved"—ready for the Second Coming. If God is going to take care of the reconstruction of society—and soon—Christians simply don't have to worry about it or do anything to help God build his Kingdom. But Bill does not operate according to this type of premillennial eschatology.

In the Campus Crusade statement of faith, the words *imminent* and *millennial* or *premillennial* are not to be found, contrary to most modern-day evangelical statements. There *is* great confidence in the life after death and the final resurrection of the dead, but the clause dealing with the Last Things is open to premillennial interpretations (without the necessity of imminency), amillennial theology (Christ will come again, but biblical millennial imagery is not to be taken literally), and even postmillennialism (in which Christ returns after the millennium). "Jesus Christ will come again to earth—personally, visibly, and bodily—to consummate history and the eternal plan of God." Unlike most evangelical evangelists, Bill is not at all interested in the urgency of evangelism in order to prepare people for the Rapture (in which, according to dispensational theology, only Christians will participate), when believers will be taken out of the world for seven years preceding the millennium, while the unbelieving and unrighteous world works its way to Armageddon. His sense of urgency, rather, is motivated by his belief that new Spirit-filled believers *en masse* can "change the world" in anticipation of the Kingdom's ultimate consummation, which cannot occur until the gospel has been preached to every creature, anyway, and may not take place for hundreds, even thousands of years. This is why Bill stresses, in addition to aggressive evangelism, discipleship training—building the *agape* person—and why he feels very comfortable planning a large graduate university that will probably take decades to emerge in full form. And this is the reason he wants 100,000 *Agape* movement volunteers by 1980, the year earmarked for the initial fulfillment of the Great Commission: a massive army of Campus Crusade people who will demonstrate even to hostile governments the power of the gospel, rooted in the fullness of the Spirit and *agape*, not only to change lives individually but to change corporate society as well.

In this connection, it is interesting to note Bill's fondness for describing positive social change and progress in communities around the world affected, for instance, by Here's Life. At the end of 1976, he explained, "As strange as it may seem in the brief time period of Here's Life so far, there are reported dramatic changes in the crime rate. For example, in Atlanta the homicide rate was reduced almost 25 percent. Other cities have also witnessed a dramatic drop. Social reforms normally come five to ten years, or even twenty-five years, after a great awakening. I anticipate that out of this great spiritual awakening [including Here's Life] will come major reforms that will affect the lives of every American and much of the world. The crime rate will be altered. And I am sure racial conflicts will be dealt with in a more Christian way. There will be a dramatic change for the better in upgrading the quality of television fare and all entertainment. In the last thirty years the trend in this country has been gradually away from the things of God, and I think there will be a gradual trend back as changed people inspired by the love of God will be doing what comes naturally. I don't think there will be a sudden confrontation [e.g., violent revolution, Armageddon]. I think changes will come because tens of millions of people on the grass roots level are turning back to God."

The issue in evangelism, therefore, is to motivate people to accept the gospel urgently, en masse, then to become salt and light in the world, changing society through good works, by the power of the Holy Spirit, to the point where the consummation of the Kingdom of God is the logical outcome, because believers will have already been partners with God in laying its foundation.

Such an eschatology is closely akin to that espoused by the nineteenth-century revivalist social reformers, most prominently Charles G. Finney, whose holiness, perfectionist, and free-will theology was an affront to strict amillennial and premillennial Calvinists. Finney, who helped lead the struggle against slavery, and many of his evangelical counterparts in the nineteenth century—including Jonathan Blanchard, first president of Wheaton College in Illinois—were effectively postmillennialists. Christ would return to earth only after the 1,000 years of righteousness and peace on earth, created by committed believers empowered for service by the Holy Spirit. Although Bill would not want to be called a postmillennialist himself—two world wars have made such a positive notion of human progress seem naive—his theology does display ideas and actions reminiscent of that position.

Of course, Bill Bright's vision, his idealism, has been tempered by the pragmatism he learned on the ranch in Oklahoma and in business, and the struggle between them in his thinking has been apparent for many years. To make Bill's vision operational and a reality, he and his top-level staff members have employed pragmatic means. Ministry, to be successful must *work*. This is the fundamental reason behind the common criticism that Campus Crusade believes the ends justify the means. It is also the reason Bill has allowed so many premillennialists and dispensationalists to join staff—not because he wants to promote any one eschatological position but rather because they have been the U.S. Christians *most* interested in his evangelistic goals and strategies. Bill's vision explains his appropriation of what the world thinks is impossible. Like John R. Mott, he insists that, for the committed Christian, the impossible is often achieved more easily than that which comes simply. And he refuses to let others, however sincere, convince him otherwise.

BILL'S IMPOSSIBLE DREAMS

On November 15, 1977, Bill Bright held a news conference in Washington, D.C., to announce his latest impossible dream—a plan to raise $1 billion by 1982 for "the most extensive Christian social and evangelization mission in recorded history." Because of the incredibly large amount of money involved in this campaign, the news conference was attended and reported on by many representatives of the secular media, who brought Bill to the attention of American religious leaders who hardly knew his name before that conference.

Details of the massive fund-raising drive include continued expansion of the Here's Life strategy to other continents; the development of four different task forces, one of which will help develop technology for reaching rural areas in Africa, Latin America, and Asia with the gospel; and a five-year campaign to raise $1 billion to finance these efforts.

Wallace E. Johnson, co-founder of Holiday Inns, Inc., is serving as international chair of the fund-raising campaign; Roy Rogers, actor and businessman, is vice-chair; and Nelson Bunker Hunt, oil executive and investor, is chair of the international executive committee. Edward Johnson, chairman and president of Financial Federated Corporation is chair of the U.S. committee. The executive committee itself consists of approximately twenty business and professional leaders who will, in turn, direct a sponsoring committee of 1,000 individuals in gathering contributions and pledges of $100 million in one year and the remaining $900 million by 1982. At the news conference, Johnson made it clear that the fund-raising operation will target potential funds not now being channeled into other Christian churches and organizations.

The other three task forces in the project will develop films and radio and television programming that will be used in both rural areas and cities; concentrate on establishing good diplomatic relations with government leaders; and coordinate Campus Crusade's evangelistic and discipleship training efforts with those of other Christian organizations and churches so as to avoid duplication.

Bill has also launched a strategy for another impossible dream—his international Christian Graduate University, still in the initial stages. Its School of Theology, opened in 1978 at Arrowhead Springs, represents the first constituent school of the university. Planning for the institution's long-range development is being led by Charles A. LeMaistre, chancellor of the University of Texas; Charles Malik, professor in the American University, Beirut, Lebanon, and former president of the United Nations General Assembly; and Harold J. Ockenga, president of Gordon-Conwell Theological Seminary and a prominent evangelical leader.

Bill Bright says that he wants his projected university to be "the very finest graduate university possible, a university of the highest academic standards, the finest spiritual emphasis. One that is truly Christian, biblically oriented, committed to Christ. The purpose of this graduate university will be to meet the needs of Christians who really want to make their witness count. Our goal will be to train leaders in all the disciplines such as law, medicine, education, business, communications, government, labor, and theology." International Christian Graduate University would be the first distinctively Christian university in the world to concentrate exclusively on graduate education.

12 Bill Bright the Conservative, Bill Bright the Radical

> Far too often the subversive world is united when we Christians are knocking each other. If we are going to have a part in changing the world, we are going to have to get our act together.
>
> VONETTE ZACHARY BRIGHT

BILL BRIGHT: HIS CHARACTER, HIS PERSONALITY, HIS LIFESTYLE

There is no such thing as a rigid routine in the life of Bill Bright. Often he works and sleeps alternately around the clock. On the more "normative" days, however, Bill gets up between 5:00 and 5:30 in the morning and begins each day with devotions—prayer and Bible study. (One of his close colleagues asserts that he is praying constantly, in everything he does.) Sometimes Bill doesn't sleep at all, especially when he has writing to catch up with, and he tries very hard to keep up with the news (his staff give him particularly important stories to digest). He finds it even more difficult to make time for much theological study, a real drawback in his ministry. Reading is often scheduled for his "spare time," of which there is very little. Bill and Vonette travel the world 90 percent of the time, spending only a few days each month in Arrowhead Springs. For most people, weekends mean some measure of relaxation, but for Bill weekends are much the same as weekdays, sometimes even busier. The word vacation isn't in his vocabulary, because he never really takes one. Bill, not unlike other religious leaders, has few close friends other than Vonette and his cabinet members. He simply hasn't the time for friends, unless friendship becomes an instrument, to help fulfill the Great Commission, one reason he pours his life into the members of his cabinet, his closest working colleagues. People can be Bill's friends only insofar as they are one with his vision and work to make that vision a reality. Priorities, a most important work to him, are always ranked by how well they fit into his one-track mind centered on fulfilling the Great Commission.

For Bill, leisure is work, and work is leisure. He has extraordinary energy, as anyone who has worked or traveled with him knows. Despite his businesslike pragmatism, the president of Campus Crusade is a very "relational" person. Bill sends a postcard to his parents in Coweta, now in their eighties, almost daily, and he phones them every week. He hurts when he hears of his staff or other Christian leaders hurting and almost always calls to offer them his help (always when tragedy, such as a death in the family, strikes his staff, who are his family). And he hurts when those he loves hurt him.

Bill is a very confident, nondependent leader. Because he is a visionary with a continual emphasis on moving ahead with urgency, he's wary of Campus Crusade's becoming ingrown and introspective. And despite Bill's relational character, he always warns his staff about the ever-present danger of their discipleship training groups turning into mere encounter or sensitivity groups. Rather, there must always be action to make the vision a reality—motivating disciples to move out in faith strong enough to move mountains. He worries that his staff will become too dependent on each other and not dependent enough on Christ. Nevertheless, Bill himself is a very vulnerable person, trusting those he knows love him implicitly, even blindly, which is one reason he's been "burned" so badly on occasion.

Many Christian leaders and others, media personnel, for instance, feel that Bill is completely insensitive to their concerns and opinions, doesn't need them, has his own plan, and is uncooperative. To a degree, this accusation is often true. On the other hand, Bill does seek out the opinions of Christian leaders and others he respects. The key to that respect, moreover, is whether those individuals are men and women of great faith or whether they more consistently express unbelief, as exhibited by thinking small rather than big. He won't criticize the latter people, but he refuses to slow down what he feels God is leading him to do in order to appease or accommodate them. Again, because Bill is a confident visionary, he leads with a sense of "Thus saith the Lord," and is often reluctant to take the advice of "just any" Christian leader, because he was criticized so severely in the early years of Campus Crusade for things that, in his opinion, proved to be valid and successful and were adopted, finally, by many, many believers (the Four Spiritual Laws, for example).

Bill is also a very spiritual man—a true pietist in the best sense of the word. Next to his vision, it is his "godliness" that keeps his staff on board. They look at his character, his lifestyle, his marriage, and his sense of personal morality and holiness, and want to emulate them. Even Bill's black staff members and colleagues greatly admire his spirituality and, more than that, his selflessness—despite their opinion, at times, that he isn't moving fast enough in implementing the social dimension of the gospel.

Bill tries very hard to be an honest, forthright, and "transparent" person, and he encourages his staff to be the same. That's why his own financial records and those of Campus Crusade are open to the scrutiny of all who need to know and some who don't need to know. Yet Bill's transparent self is in conflict with the man's inherent mystique, the quality of his personality that remains hidden until you know his heart. And you can't really know Bill Bright until you know his heart.

Bill Bright's background, personality, associations, vision, and pragmatism have all contributed to the basic character of Campus Crusade and to the way it is perceived from the outside. And Bill himself is the root cause of many of the criticisms, valid and invalid, made of the organization.

The name *Campus Crusade for Christ* itself has been criticized because of its military overtones. The Crusades were nothing that Christians would brag about today. During the last several decades, military language has been pervasive throughout evangelical revivalism and evangelism as a whole in such words as *crusade, campaign, rally, enlist, win, retreat, advance, prayer warrior,* and unique in Campus Crusade, *blitz, saturation, front, capturing the campus,* and *Great Commission Army*. This vocabulary emerged prior to the Vietnam conflict within circles that were, in fact, very promilitary in their orientation. Today its popularity, even within evangelical churches and movements, has diminished considerably, and it is unlikely that Campus Crusade would have selected that name had the organization been founded in the late 1970s rather than in 1951, when Americans were still celebrating the victories of World War II.

Aggressive evangelism also has been criticized because it seems offensive to some, and its primary focus is on numbers, seemingly at the cost of neglecting long-term, loving relationships with those who make a decision for Christ. Bill, of course, insists that aggressive evangelism does mean taking the initiative, the offense, but not being offensive. Campus Crusade does emphasize numbers—of people who have heard the gospel through its work, made decisions, enrolled in follow-up activities, and joined staff. And numbers do indicate success to Bill. The more converts the better. Numbers also indicate to him the degree to which the Great Commission has been fulfilled. Nevertheless, he argues that people won through the ministry of Campus Crusade are encouraged and helped to take the next step, to become disciples.

Many people regard the Four Spiritual Laws (or *principles* if *laws* seem offensive) as a vehicle for "instant salvation," almost as easy as buying a hamburger at McDonald's. Bill is convinced that salvation is to be found easily, because it is rooted entirely in God's grace not in human effort, in works. Yet anyone who really knows Bill or his staff also knows that receiving Christ through the Four Spiritual Laws is only the beginning. Nothing short of 100 percent commitment to Christ as a disciple can lead to Christian maturity. Bill has a profound sense of simplicity both in his theology and in the methodology he uses to convey it. He likes to take abstract, complex, and often confusing concepts and simplify them—getting right to the heart of the issue, making the issue "transferable" so that it can change the world. Bill sees many Christian leaders who have been trying to convince people for years to become Christians in sophisticated theological and metaphysical abstractions, without success. But he feels that "four spiritual principles," "nine transferable concepts,"

and "ten basic steps" are a simpler and better way to reach people
and help them understand the gospel.

Jesus also had a kind of simplicity about him. Unlike the Pharisees,
he got down to the basics. When people pressed him for one
comprehensive rule, he told them, "You shall love the Lord your God
with all your heart, and with all your soul, and with all your
mind . . . [and] you shall love your neighbor as yourself" (Matthew
22:37, 39, NASB). Today most people are in a rush. They demand
simple answers yet true answers. If men and women are looking for
God, they are no longer satisfied with abstract, complicated hints or
clues on how to find him and how to behave in the process. Thus the
Four Spiritual Laws—which have gone through a succession of
revisions since their inception to make them culturally relevant—
have provided a way to find God simply and quickly (many people
do like McDonald's hamburgers). And despite the accusation that
they are simplistic, Bill Bright feels that they've worked and that
they've worked well. And for him, that's the ultimate issue.

The criticism, however, that Campus Crusade's follow-up and
discipleship training materials are inadequate because their chief
focus is how to win others and how to live a spiritual life, neglecting
the concrete social-ethical demands of the gospel, is more valid. At
present, Christian social concern is almost entirely omitted from
these training materials, which stress the vertical relationship to God
much more than the horizontal relationship to one's neighbor and to
the world, despite the fact that, at its core, the gospel is 100 percent
personal and 100 percent social. The ethical teachings of Jesus in the
synoptic gospels and the social-ethical concerns of the Old Testament
prophets are hardly discussed at all.

But Campus Crusade is no more guilty of this omission than most
twentieth-century evangelicals who have only recently discovered
the social dimension of the gospel, and Bill's evangelical colleagues
outside the movement haven't helped him with this problem at all.
Nevertheless, at the urging of Campus Crusade's Latin American
staff and others within the movement, change is coming. A strong
social action component is being placed in the new standardized
cross-cultural training curriculum—building the *agape* person—that

all movement staff will study in the future. And perhaps the time has come for Bill himself to write another transferable concept to convince his own staff and the critics that he does take the social dimension of the gospel seriously. Verbal witness, as his black staff members have told him, is simply not enough. And the Lausanne Covenant makes that very clear as well.

Bill's unabashed use of the mass media in evangelism has already been discussed at some length as his pragmatic way to reach the largest number of people possible with the essentials of the gospel. His critics, especially those who, in their hearts, at least, also believe in fulfilling the Great Commission, should take a closer look at this strategy. Maybe it is the best way to proceed in our generation. Maybe, in fact, it does work. (The late Pope John Paul I suggested that if Jesus had come to earth in our generation he probably would have worked for one of the international wire services.) What seems crassly superficial to some people clearly doesn't seem superficial to the multitudes of individuals who have responded to this method of evangelism and have been changed in the process.

The same can be said of those ever-present smiles on the faces of Campus Crusade staff. Superficial? Plastic? In a few cases, probably so. But the fact is that most staff members smile because they *are* happy, and this is probably the primary reason so many people have responded positively to their message on the one-to-one level. Critics might well change their minds if they took the time to get to know, and even befriend, the Campus Crusade staff members they feel are superficial. Nothing breaks a false stereotype more effectively than friendship.

Bill Bright has the reputation of being an authoritarian leader. It is certainly the case that Campus Crusade is structured around a clearly defined chain of command with Bill at the top. But, as mentioned earlier, the movement is better understood as a family than as a mere religious organization modeled after a corporation. In fact, much more freedom is available to staff than is generally conceded. Despite his critics' assertions to the contrary, Bill is a teachable person, who, by and large, is open to any evangelistic and discipleship training strategy that he is convinced will work well to help fulfill the Great Commission in our generation. He does not pry into the private lives and lifestyles of his staff, because he trusts them to not offend their "weaker" brothers and sisters and to lead the kind of life that will be an example to the world of the best Christian character. Bill does, however, expect total commitment from each staff person. Campus Crusade is organized in such a way that only those staff members who are completely committed to its overall goals and strategies can find real fulfillment in their ministries within the movement. Illegitimate and repressive authority must be challenged, but there can be no true freedom, no "liberation," with authority, as described so well by the prophetic words of songwriter Kris Kristofferson in "Lovin' Arms": "Lookin' back and longing for the freedom of my chains." No organization with goals as big as Campus Crusade's can carry them out apart from leaders who have and wield authority in humane and constructive ways. By and large, Bill and his top leadership try very hard to exercise that authority over the family in an affirming and loving way.

A major contradiction within Campus Crusade, mentioned earlier, is the role of women in the organization. Despite Bill's and Vonette's public statements to the contrary, women's role and authority within the movement have been severely restricted. Almost always—in the major ministries, in any case—women evangelize and disciple women, not men. Most often they have no spiritual authority over men in any context, and only rarely are they given any kind of authority over men, especially in the U.S. field. Just a handful of women hold top leadership posts, and very few minister from regular "line" (rather than "staff") positions leading to advancement up the ladder. Only on the rarest occasions have women been given the title of campus director of ministry, except at women's colleges in the United States and in a few countries abroad. And never has a woman been an area or regional director of campus ministry. Vonette, who is the one woman on the movement's board of directors, is also the only woman in the cabinet, although she rarely attends.

The problem has nothing to do with theology. Bill and Vonette both affirm the ordination of women and the possibility of their equal participation with men in church and society and within

Campus Crusade. Then why the contradiction? Because Bill's idealism, his vision, says yes, while pragmatism says no. Women should be equal, but, pragmatically speaking, Bill is afraid that women with authority, especially spiritual authority, over men will make men not want to participate with them at all. Furthermore, he doesn't wish to offend whole denominations that exclude women from leadership and some of his own male staff who feel strongly that women should submit entirely to men without reservation. And when Vonette publicly announces that she preaches in church pulpits with her husband's full authority, and only by his authority, she forgets that most evangelical husbands would never allow their wives to preach or even to teach men, except children in Sunday school, perhaps. Their churches teach against it.

In the movement's campus ministry, husband-wife, man-woman teamwork in ministry has been emphasized ever since Bill and Vonette started the work together in 1951. But despite the fact that women do as much of the same type of work as men do, they are not generally regarded as true equals either within or from outside the movement. In a marital team relationship, the husband is almost always the dominant minister and the focal point when it comes to relationships in ministry, again, both within and outside the movement. Furthermore, despite Campus Crusade's self-understanding as a family, there is very little feeling of *sisterhood* among women staff, while the men have a powerful sense of brotherhood that reflects a profound spiritual relationship. Men call each other *brother*, but it is rare for women to use the word *sister* in that sense. Thus Campus Crusade tends to be a family of dominant brothers and submissive sisters.

Nevertheless, an increasing number of women within the movement are no longer content to "keep in their place" for fear of putting down the male ego. This minority of women staff—who still keep their opinions largely to themselves—feel strongly that women who are otherwise qualified should not only be considered for leadership positions, they should be encouraged to work toward greater leadership within Campus Crusade. At present there are a number of women in the U.S. campus ministry who already *function* (without the title) as campus directors of ministry with spiritual authority over both men and women, mainly at two-year community colleges, where men are less likely to want to go. It is clear that, with the general advancement of women's equality in our society, the situation within Campus Crusade and in other similar religious movements will change. But it probably won't change at a fast rate until the organization's women staff together demand equal treatment and equal opportunity, in a constructive manner understandable to Bill. The Bible does not defend the preservation of the male ego; rather, it conveys true liberation for all people, and encourages men and women, husbands and wives, to become mutually submissive to each other in Christ. This is the only way a man-woman team ministry can really be successful. Christians must learn to understand that they are not just sons of Abraham, Isaac, and Jacob but daughters of Abigail, Priscilla, and Sarah as well.

The problem of the role of women in Campus Crusade is one reflection of an even deeper problem within the movement—the lack of effective self-criticism, or, in the organization's vocabulary, *self-evaluation*. Despite the fact that there are a number of official and unofficial channels for constructive criticism within Campus Crusade, including an extensive annual survey of the staff members' feelings about a variety of subjects, the overarching policy of noncriticism of other Christian movements and leaders actually mitigates against self-criticism. That policy is surely a good one in principle, but it tends to make staff uncomfortable at best and guilty at worst when they are seen to complain about their grievances, even in an authorized and proper manner. Thus many staff members simply keep quiet about their criticisms until their ministries suffer, then they quit, but rarely admit the real reasons for their departure. Consequently, the movement never finds out the truth and continues to believe that its present course is satisfactory and no change is required. In fact, Bill is open to constructive criticism, from within Campus Crusade especially, and needs to hear that criticism personally if other established channels of redress prove to be ineffective.

Another contradiction within the movement has to do with culture and lifestyle more generally—in a word, with pietism. Dean M.

Kelley, author of *Why Conservative Churches are Growing* and director for civil and religious liberty of the National Council of Churches, pointed out in a series of lectures given at Texas Christian University in 1978 the strengths and weaknesses of pietism. On the positive side, pietism has stood for (1) each person's direct experience of salvation; (2) a high view of biblical authority; and (3) the necessity of leading a fully Christian life marked by ethical sensitivity, evangelistic and missionary zeal, mutual upbearing in small groups, and a strong lay initiative in ministry. On the negative side, however, pietism has tended to foster (1) elitism; (2) legalism; (3) introspection; (4) separation; and (5) and extreme "spiritualization" of values. As a pietist himself, Bill stands for all the best in pietism, and he soundly condemns its weaknesses. Nevertheless, it has been very difficult for him to divorce himself from the pietistic tendencies toward legalism and super-spirituality, despite his words to the contrary.

Bill wants the gospel proclaimed and demonstrated by his staff to be culturally relevant, which is why he has given the maximum amount of freedom in ministry to his U.S. minority staff and his international staff. He knows that the recent tradition of "white pietism" with its abhorrence of all worldly pleasures (including dancing, drinking, smoking, and card playing) in favor of "spiritual" activities alone (prayer, worship, and verbal witness, with regular Bible study) simply will not work within the U.S. black community and within European culture, for instance. What Bill hasn't realized yet is that modern American white Christians have also rejected, to a large degree, the traditional taboos inherent in recent white pietism. Since the 1960s, fewer Christians in the United States, including evangelicals, are offended by their brothers and sisters who feel that they can be authentic and faithful believers and still have a good time. Bill needs to understand that if his staff in Europe are allowed to fully participate in their culture, which is one reason the staff turnover rate there is so low, Americans should be allowed in good conscience to do the same. Many highly talented individuals who would otherwise welcome the opportunity to serve on Campus Crusade's staff in this country don't even consider it because of what appear to be irrelevant restrictions on their personal cultural behavior that has nothing to do with the quality of their spirituality. Furthermore, present staff who do drink on occasion, for example, tend to live with deep feelings of guilt, not because they are breaking a rule, but because they know that Bill simply doesn't like it. And when their guilt becomes too great, they quit staff.

Pietists often have tended to be so spiritual, so "heavenly minded," that they're no earthly good. All material pleasures become an evil in themselves, and even love is spiritualized. Love may be an attitude of the heart, but it is inadequately demonstrated in action. This is a fundamental weakness in Bill's concept of loving by faith. For one can easily love his or her enemies "by faith" without any concrete demonstration of that love. It is therefore meaningless, because, in the favorite words of the *Agape* movement, love is something you do. Undemonstrated love is inadequate, because one *can* love by faith *and* demonstrate that love. It means, rather, that loving by faith, wrongly interpreted—without the necessary action component—is simply not love at all.

Bill's unconscious tendency as a pietist toward legalism and overspiritualization of values is something he honestly tries to avoid, because that legalism and spiritualization of values has no place in his own theology. Fellow Christian leaders as well as his top-echelon staff members need to help him recognize and suppress this tendency.

POLITICS

Nothing about Bill Bright has been criticized so severely as his politics or, more accurately perhaps, the world's perception of his politics. Bill is a "bimodal thinker," to use the concept of semanticist S. I. Hayakawa—a person who tends to see the world in mutually exclusive categories like right or wrong, good or bad, appropriate or inappropriate, timely or untimely, and ultimately, cold white or black. There is no in-between possibility in his thinking. Thus when staff insiders or those on the outside see the world as a much more complex entity than that, they become very frustrated with Bill.

When Bill considers the overall effect of Here's Life, for instance, it has been 100 percent successful, not just 85, 70, or 60 percent successful. The same thing holds true in regard to his feelings about his closest staff members, who report to him directly. Either they have his full confidence, or they don't have his confidence at all. In the latter case, there are many creative and highly motivated people outside the movement today simply because they lost Bill's confidence. He cannot live with shades of gray. This attitude also colors his politics. Bill thinks that his evangelism and discipleship training are not politically motivated, because to be politically motivated one has to be 100 percent involved in politics, endorsing and promoting candidates, lobbying, being an active party worker, and the like. Because he stops short of those activities in his speeches and writings, he's not politically motivated. (Indeed, all Campus Crusade staff must stop short of such political involvement.)

With respect to his own political position, however, Bill explains, "I have rejected labels just as I have done in theology. In some ways, I'd probably be considered very conservative, and in other ways very liberal. I am opposed to big government, because I think it destroys people. When we do *everything* for people, we don't help them at all. Personally, I would favor the kind of government aid that helps and encourages people to help themselves. I'm very much concerned about the poor and the disenfranchised, but I don't think that big government—with its enormous waste of money and manpower—can help them effectively. *De*centralization of government is a better answer, in which authority and power is really brought to the people, to the masses."

"The fact of the matter," he goes on to say, "is that 45 percent of our people are functionally illiterate. And millions of Americans are still on welfare and in need of food, decent shelter, and basic health care. This is an incredible and inexcusable injustice, but there has to be a better way to solve the problem than the dole system. To my mind, that better system would be one based upon Christian concern and compassion. Contrary to common belief, I never urge the election of 'Christian leaders' per se, because many well-intentioned Christians simply don't have the ability, or even the integrity, to run our nation. Rather, I'd like to see qualified 'men and women of God' elected to public office. If there are enough people in government who seek first the Kingdom of God and base their decisions on biblical principles, then we'd have a better government and a better country."

Bill's basically conservative politics, of course, are the product of his boyhood in Coweta, Oklahoma, his brief but successful career in business, and his politically conservative friends and colleagues, among them, former Congress member from Minnesota Walter H. Judd, a committed anticommunist who wrote the foreword to Bill's book, *Come Help Change the World*, published in 1970; arch-conservative Senator Strom Thurmond; and former Representative from Arizona John Conlan, another very conservative Republican. Add to these the numerous politically conservative evangelical leaders with whom Bill travels; other notable right-wingers like Richard DeVos, president of Amway corporation; and Campus Crusade board members Arlis Priest, L. Allen Morris, and S. Elliot Belcher. It is interesting to note that Bill seemingly has very few politically liberal friends or associates.

The *Sojourners* exposé of April 1976 was written by its young radical evangelical editor, Jim Wallis (another bimodal thinker) and managing editor Wes Michaelson, Senator Mark Hatfield's former executive assistant. They utilized a number of pieces of evidence to put together their conspiracy theory, starting with Bill's long history of right-wing associations and his speeches and writings of the 1950s, 1960s, and 1970s that appear politically conservative and anticommunist. In his book, *Revolution Now*, published in 1969, Bill declares that "the diabolical manipulations of international communism are bringing us ever closer to universal tyranny." And one close associate of Bright says that he was "to the right of Barry Goldwater" in 1964. Other evidence used by *Sojourners* was the seemingly clear interrelationship of people associated with the Christian Embassy, the Campus Crusade board of directors, and the Christian Freedom Foundation and Third Century Publishers (founded in 1974 to publish books and other materials to articulate an ideologically conservative political and economic philosophy allegedly based on biblical principles). Art De Moss of the Campus Crusade board told *Sojourners*, "There is so much mutual interest and overlap between people, in Campus Crusade for Christ, the Christian Embassy, Third Century Publishers, and the Christian Freedom Foundation, that it is very hard for me to keep it all straight."

According to Wallis and Michaelson, Conlan and DeVos organized a national effort through the Christian Freedom Foundation in 1976 to elect "real Christians" (i.e., political conservatives) to government through fund-raising activities, neighborhood political canvassing, and distribution of works by Third Century Publishers.

It is manifestly clear that a conspiracy of some sort was being planned by people associated with the aforementioned organizations and with Bill himself. Because Bill attended a crucial meeting organized by these people, endorsed a book published by Third Century entitled *In the Spirit of '76,* and had an article by John Conlan talking about his "plan" and listing the address of Third Century Publishers for more information in the December 1975 issued of *Worldwide Challenge, Sojourners* assumed that he not only knew about the conspiracy but was, in fact, part of it. Bill, of course, denies his involvement, and it does appear that he was the victim of guilt by association. An extremely busy man, Bill attends innumerable meetings day in and day out, and he claims that he didn't even understand what was going on in that meeting. With respect to the book endorsement, he hadn't even read the book. A staff member read it, liked it, and suggested that Bill endorse it. (When Steve Douglass saw that endorsement, he almost fell out of his chair.) And Bill also claims that he didn't know what Third Century Publishers was really about until he read the *Sojourners* article. Furthermore, Campus Crusade might have lost everything if Bill had been part of the conspiracy, because it would have contradicted their own policy of severely limiting staff political involvement. Bill had too much to lose. In the end, moreover, Conlan lost his seat in Congress by running unsuccessfuly for the Senate from Arizona in 1976; even Barry Goldwater, another conservative Republican, refused to endorse his candidacy. Perhaps that tells something about the matter in question.

The tragedy is that, like Bill, Wallis and Michaelson are evangelical Christians. Although their intentions of finding out the truth in
this case were admirable, they were wrong about Bill's intentions,
though probably correct about the intentions and actions of some of
the other people involved. The fact that both Jim Wallis and Bill
Bright are bimodal thinkers, of different political persuasions, is one
reason they can't get along. But Bill's words indicate where he is
now: "I love Jim Wallis, and I've thought of spending some time
with him to say, if you really are committed believers and really
want to enhance the Kingdom and help fulfill the Great Commission, I'm with you. Let's not cut each other down. Instead, let's work
together in harmony and love." This is a rather amazing statement
by a man who felt strongly that *Sojourners* was trying to destroy
Campus Crusade in an incident that was one of the most troublesome
things that ever happened to him.

Insiders know that Bill can be very naive politically. One of his
closest associates had to demonstrate to him, on a blackboard, that his
"nonpolitical stance" really was political; it didn't appear neutral at
all but rang conservative. Bill was amazed. Furthermore, it is also
apparent that Bill's stance is changing. Some of his own European
staff members, socialists and others among them, have complained
about his public positions on politics that seem so very right-wing in
character. They can't be involved in politics, so why should Bill? Bill
was as happy to accept the invitation to preach in a communist
country, the Soviet Union, as he was to hold Explo '74 in an
anticommunist country, South Korea. Since the invitation, approved
by the government, came from the recognized Baptist Christians
there, Bill was hit hard by his anticommunist colleagues and supporters who look upon the leaders of the recognized churches as secret
police, KGB agents. But he went anyway, determined to "love the
Russian people," and gave such a glowing report at his Moscow news
conference that his staff had to help him put together a "more
realistic" report for official purposes. Bill also hosted three Soviet
Baptist ministers in this country for a tour of Campus Crusade's
operation, at the movement's expense. And Bill's task force on
diplomatic relations associated with the billion-dollar fund-raising

campaign will help him avoid partisan politics in the future. The irony of Bill's history of anticommunism—motivated not for economic reasons but rather because he is skeptical about religious freedom in communist countries—is that Campus Crusade, like very few other religious organizations in the United States, is run on the principle "from each according to his ability, to each according to his need."

When the Reverend Joon Gon Kim, director of Campus Crusade for Christ in South Korea, was interviewed by columnist Jack Anderson after Explo '74, he lamented the imprisonment of his fellow Korean Christians by President Park for political reasons. These are "liberation Christians," Kim said, who believe strongly that the church must side with the oppressed and work to change society. Most Korean Christians agree, he continued, yet they also believe that the church should stay out of politics. Unfortunately, Kim concluded, "It is difficult to draw the line betwen religious action and political action." The majority of Christians in South Korea, he said, would draw the line at violence. With those comments, Joon Gon Kim sounds more like Jim Wallis than Bill Bright. As Campus Crusade's ministries move more and more into countries with totalitarian regimes of both the left and the right, it may become almost impossible for them to always take a totally neutral political stance in those nations. The movement's staff are highly committed people who would risk their lives to protect their disciples. The world may never be able to appreciate Campus Crusade's and Bill Bright's commitment to social justice until its first staff member is jailed in one of those lands or deported for "political" reasons—when resistance, as in Nazi Germany, is no longer an optional political act, but a religious obligation.

ECUMENISM AND THE GREAT COMMISSION

Bill and Vonette founded Campus Crusade for Christ as a servant of the church, and it is only in that context that the movement's true significance can be discerned. In the last several years, the so-called mainline American denominations have suffered dramatic losses in membership in general and even more striking losses of young people in particular. As a result, evangelism has become a major priority in almost all of these denominations as well as in the National Council of Churches and the World Council of Churches. At its 1975 General Assembly in Nairobi, the WCC adopted a powerful report on "Confessing Christ Today," reaffirming the church's evangelistic mandate in an increasingly secular world. This report declares:

> We *deplore* conversions without witness to Christ. There are millions who have never heard the good news. We *confess* that we are often ashamed of the gospel. We find it more comfortable to remain in our own Christian circles than to witness in the world. . . . In confessing Christ and in being converted to his Lordship, we experience the freedom of the Holy Spirit and express the ultimate hope for the world.

Likewise, in 1976, the governing board of the National Council of Churches adopted an official policy statement on evangelism, the proclamation and demonstration of the good news that Jesus Christ came into the world to reconcile sinners to God. That statement concludes by saying:

> The task of evangelism today is calling people to repentance, to faith in Jesus Christ, to study God's word, to continue steadfast in prayer, and to bearing witness to him. This is a primary function of the church in its congregational, denominational and ecumenical manifestations. . . . Now, after the journey of the past twenty-five years [the NCC's history], we can call upon people to confess the Name of Jesus Christ and bear witness to that Name in their lives with a fuller understanding of Christian discipleship and a deeper commitment to share the Good News we have found.

Probably no organization in the world is better equipped to assist the church in its evangelistic outreach than Campus Crusade. Bill has made his movement extremely accessible to the needs of the church because of its unabashed ecumenical character. *Ecumenical* is not a dirty word. Derived from the Greek *oikoumene,* the inhabited earth, it signifies a call for the oneness and unity of the Body of Christ "that the world may believe" (John 17:21, NASB). Thus ecumenism and evangelism go together. Campus Crusade, with its character of being a servant of the church, its teachable attitude, its policy of noncriticism, its repudiation of dogmatism, its emphasis on unconditional love, and its focus on the work of the Holy Spirit—the agent of all Christian unity—can help the church at all levels do its evangelistic task effectively, make mature disciples of its members, and send them out to win, build, and send others still. If Campus Crusade hasn't loved the church enough, it is probably because the church hasn't loved Campus Crusade at all.

The church needs Campus Crusade to regain the motivation of the first-century disciples to win the world with a sense of urgency in anticipation of the coming Kingdom of God. And Campus Crusade needs the church to train new and mature believers in the faith that can move mountains. The Great Commission can never be fulfilled in this or any generation until the church accepts it without reservation as its mandate.

Bill Bright *is*, in many ways, a true conservative. But in terms of his vision, he is nothing less than a radical—motivated by *agape*, the root of Christian faith, and the quality of life that represents a fundamental departure from the world system and its characteristic way of doing things. Bill will probably never in his own lifetime be widely regarded as a saint. Nevertheless, despite all his weaknesses, Bill's faith and, more than that, his vision should inspire the church to again attempt the impossible with confidence, just as Christ commanded his followers 2,000 years ago. Fulfilling the Great Commission in our generation, humanly speaking, is an impossibility. But when we are convinced that with God *nothing* is impossible, and when we undertake his work in the world with that kind of faith, we catch sight of the greatest impossibility of all and are able to move toward it with assurance that God will indeed make it come to pass— "new heavens and a new earth wherein dwelleth righteousness" (II Peter 3:13).

Selected References

In writing this book, I have made use of officially arranged interviews with Bill Bright, Vonette Zachary Bright, Swede Anderson, Larry Benton, John Bruce, Judy Downs Douglass, Steve Douglass, Ralph Drollinger, Dave Hannah, Ron Jenson, Kalevi Lehtinen, Larry Poland, Willie Richardson, and Sergio Garcia Romo; as well as interviews with other present and former Campus Crusade staff members; and promotional brochures published by Campus Crusade. Published sources are listed below.

Athletes in Action. San Bernardino, California: Campus Crusade for Christ, 1977.

Baldwin, Ethel May, and David V. Benson. *Henrietta Mears.* Glendale, California: G/L Publications, 1966.

Bright, Bill, *Come Help Change the World.* Old Tappan, New Jersey: Revell, 1970.

——. "Door Interview: Bill Bright," *The Wittenburg Door* (February–March 1977), pp. 6–23, 26.

——. *Have You Heard of the Four Spiritual Laws?* San Bernardino, California: Campus Crusade for Christ, 1965.

——. *Have You Made the Wonderful Discovery of the Spirit-filled Life?* San Bernardino, California: Campus Crusade for Christ, 1966.

——. *A Movement of Miracles.* San Bernardino, California: Campus Crusade for Christ, 1977.

——. *Paul Brown Letter.* San Bernardino, California: Campus Crusade for Christ, 1963.

——. *Revolution Now.* San Bernardino, California: Campus Crusade for Christ, 1969.

——. *Ten Basic Steps to Christian Maturity,* 10 vols. San Bernardino, California: Campus Crusade for Christ, 1968.

————. *Transferable Concept Series*, 9 vols. San Bernardino, California: Campus Crusade for Christ, 1971–1972.

————. *Van Dusen Letter*. San Bernardino, California: Campus Crusade for Christ, 1959.

Bright, Vonette Zachary. *For Such a Time as This*. Old Tappan, New Jersey: Revell, 1976.

Campus Crusade for Christ. *Annual Report 1977*. San Bernardino, California: Campus Crusade for Christ, 1977.

————. *Campus Ministry Manual*. San Bernardino, California: Campus Crusade for Christ, 1974.

Dayton, Donald W. *Discovering an Evangelical Heritage*. New York: Harper & Row, 1976.

Douglass, Judy Downs. *Old Maid Is a Dirty Word*. San Bernardino, California: Campus Crusade for Christ, 1977.

Eshleman, Paul. *The Explo Story*. Glendale, California: G/L Publications, 1972.

Kelley, Dean M. "Four Lectures on 'Pietism.'" New York: Dean M. Kelley, 1978.

"The Lausanne Covenant." Minneapolis: Billy Graham Evangelistic Association, 1974.

Mathews, Basil, *John R. Mott: World Citizen*. New York: Harper & Row, 1934.

National Council of Churches. "A Policy Statement: Evangelism Today." New York: National Council of Churches, 1976.

Quebedeaux, Richard. *The Worldly Evangelicals*. San Francisco: Harper & Row, 1978.

Wallis, Jim, and Wes Michaelson. "The Plan to Save America," *Sojourners* (April 1976), pp. 3–12.

Whether We Live or Die. San Bernardino, California: Campus Crusade for Christ, 1977.

World Council of Churches. "Confessing Christ Today," *Breaking Barriers: Nairobi 1975*. Grand Rapids, Michigan: Eerdmans, 1976, pp. 43–57.

Worldwide Challenge (formerly *Worldwide Impact* and *Collegiate Challenge*). San Bernardino, California: Campus Crusade for Christ, 1967–1978.

Index

DATE DUE